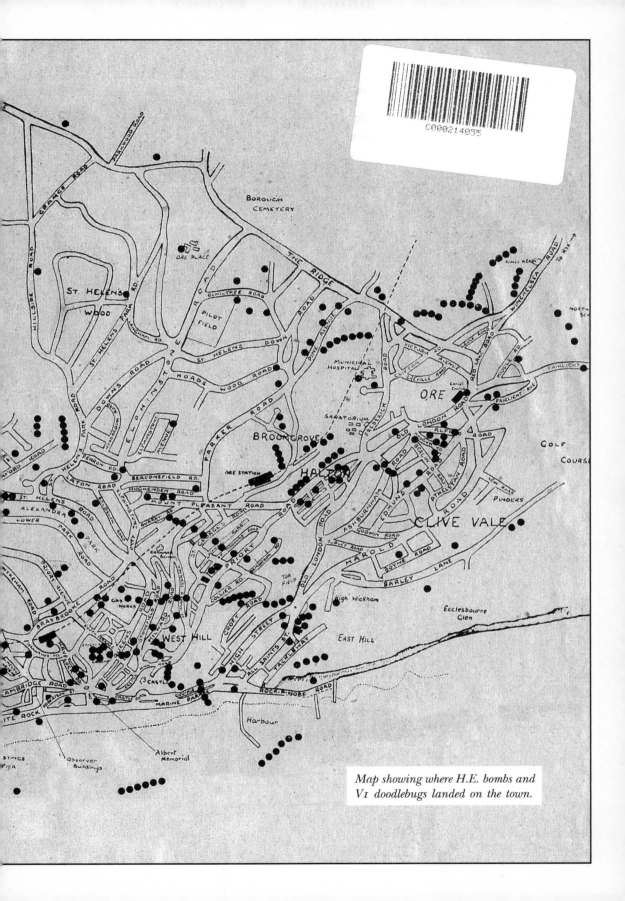

Map showing where H.E. bombs and VI doodlebugs landed on the town.

To Andy,
love Cheryl -Colin
Oct. 2005

HASTINGS AT WAR
1939-1945

Sea Road Bofors Guns.

HASTINGS AT WAR
1939-1945

Nathan Dylan Goodwin

Phillimore

2005

Published by
PHILLIMORE & CO. LTD,
Shopwyke Manor Barn, Chichester, West Sussex, England

ISBN 1 86077 328 1

Printed and bound in Great Britain by
MPG BOOKS LTD
Bodmin, Cornwall

for Robert John Bristow

CONTENTS

List of Illustrations

ACKNOWLEDGEMENTS

I would like to extend my thanks to the following people, who have all helped with the completion of this book in a variety of ways: Kevin Boorman, Sue Bower, Robert Bristow, Stan Edwards, Jane and Denis Goodwin, Anita Kennard, Andreas Nowak, Jenny Perkins, Wendy Skinner and Inge Weyergang.

My sincere thanks also go to the following, who have very kindly supplied photographs and/or given specialist information about various aspects of the war: Michael Beard and the *Hastings & St Leonards Observer*, 1, 2, 3, 17, 26, 33, 40, 42, 50, 55, 61, 64, 66, 74, 76, 78, 84 and frontispiece; John Braga; Ken Brooks, 36, 43, 58, 59, 60, 65; Chris Goss, 56; Peter Hibbs; George Humphrey; Chris Newton, 68; Andy Saunders, 23, 24, 35, 45, 47, 51, 52, 53, 57; Hastings Reference Library staff, 80, 82, 85; the staff of Hastings Museum and the Royal National Lifeboat Institution, 9.

In particular I would like to thank the contributors for their war memories and photographs, which, juxtaposed with the sombre facts and historical information, help to bring the book to life for those who are fortunate enough not to have experienced war at first-hand: Carol and Lew Boorman; Les Breach; Terry Breeds, 15; Brian Bristow, 73; John Bristow, 63; Charles Clark; Gordon and Sheila Dengate, 14, 37; Norman and Joyce Dengate, 32, 39, 81, 83; Eveline Edwards, 28, 29, 38; Joan Fincham; Bob Gearing, 71; Brenda Glazier; Frank Gutsell; Jack Hilder; Margaret Humphrey; Brenda Hunt; Derek Hutchinson; Ken Jones; June Kemp; Beryl Latimer; Dennis Layell, 6; Marjory Manton B.E.M.; Hilda Marden, 30; Derek Marsh, 49; Iona Muggridge, 20; Annette and Cathleen Munn; Ronald Ollington; M. Desmond Paine; Eileen Parish, 10, 21; Ken Perkins, 4, 11, 12, 13; Patricia Pockett; Maisie Pocock, 16; Joan Rider, 7; Peggy Smith; The Lady Soames D.B.E.; Olga Walker, 5; Brenda Wallis, 8, 22; Cecilie Warren, 79; Joyce Wedge, 72; and Dorothy Wellings.

Where no credit is given for photographs, they are the author's own. Every effort has been made to seek copyright permission for the photographs used in this book.

ABBREVIATIONS

A.A.   Anti-Aircraft
A.R.P.   Air Raid Precautions
Fw.   Feldwebel (Luftwaffe rank)
Gefr.   Gefreiter (Luftwaffe rank)
H.E.   High Explosive
Oblt.   Oberleutnant (Luftwaffe rank)
R.A.F.   Royal Air Force
R.O.C.   Royal Observer Corps
R.N.L.I.   Royal National Lifeboat Institution
V.E. Day   Victory in Europe Day
V.J. Day   Victory in Japan Day

INTRODUCTION

The idea for this book came about whilst researching the Dengate family tree in Hastings Library. Searching through the original wartime editions of the *Hastings & St Leonards Observer*, I became enthralled by a period of history in which I was interested thanks to recollections from my grandparents and Sunday afternoon black and white war films. However, I did realise that my knowledge of the town in which I was born and grew up during this time was fairly limited, and my desire to know more escalated as I read on through the newspapers: so the idea for the book was born.

The book aims to reflect what life was like in Hastings, a 'front line' town, during the years of the Second World War. The vicissitudes imposed upon the town were as sudden as they were dramatic, with the implementation of the blackout, the coastal ban, the curfew, rationing, the receiving of evacuees, and the voluntary evacuation of the town, which reduced its population by two thirds. Then came the inexorable bombing raids day and night, often with little or no warning, which left in their wake a trail of death, destruction and uncertainty and apprehension about when the next attack might occur.

I have undertaken research into the town covering many different records at national, regional and local levels. These include surviving A.R.P. records, the *Hastings & St Leonards Observer*, national newspapers, council records, and government records, which are interspersed with the very real, sometimes humorous, and often frightening accounts of those who experienced life in the town during this terrible time. I hope this will help give those who, like myself, grew up in Hastings long after the war ended a sense of what was endured during this arduous time. Though I cannot hope to represent the experiences of all people present in Hastings during the war years, it is my intention to convey an insightful account of what are certainly almost six of the most momentous years in the borough's history. I have also used many photographs to help bring the past to life, some of which have never been published before. The one common thread which runs through the interviews with Hastings residents was a great sense of neighbourliness and kindness to others – the town's folk were 'in it together', something which, to their credit, helped the town through one of the darkest phases in its history.

Although the focus of the book is Hastings and St Leonards, there are also references to the neighbouring villages of Fairlight, Westfield, Crowhurst, and Winchelsea.

Please use the email hastingswar@tiscali.co.uk to leave any feedback and also if you are able to contribute any further photographs, information or memories to any future editions of this book.

NATHAN DYLAN GOODWIN, 2005

One

In Preparation for War 1938-1939

The prospect of a protracted and costly war, which would come to affect Hastings deeply, could not have been anticipated as the political situation in Europe slowly worsened throughout the late 1930s. As early as 1935 Hastings had established an A.R.P. Committee, brought about by a letter to the Hastings Corporation from the Home Office, dated 6 July 1935. This letter was sent to boroughs 'which might be subject to attack by hostile aircraft'.[1] The threat posed to the town was considered to be high due to its close proximity to mainland Europe. By December 1937, after several meetings of the A.R.P. Committee, it was decided that the north-west stand of the Bathing Pool should be converted into the Central Distribution Station of the A.R.P., which would house all necessary equipment. First aid posts were also erected at the Bathing Pool, White Rock Baths, Tower Road Schools, Ore School and Priory Road School.[2] Such meetings of the A.R.P. Committee continued throughout the ensuing months, with the requisite precautions gradually coming into effect. The town, and indeed the country, was feeling a general apathy to the possibility of war, many believing there would be no war at all.[3]

On Saturday 29 January 1938, Hastings got its first taste of what was to come when the R.A.F. launched two mock attacks on Hastings and St Leonards. The first was a bombing raid and the second, from which the town would mercifully be spared throughout the hostilities, was a gas attack. The 'attack' was designed to test the communication and abilities of the Special Constabulary, the A.R.P. wardens, St John Ambulance Brigade, British Red Cross, and a section of the 5th (Cinque Ports) Battalion of the Sussex Regiment.[4] The mock attack seemed to have passed with only limited success. One commentator in the *Hastings & St Leonards Observer* wrote that, 'It is still difficult to get folk to grasp the need for preparation … that the lines on which the aircraft worked served rather as an advertisement for the Bathing Pool'.[5] The official report into the exercise was given to the A.R.P. Committee on 24 February 1938 and noted 'that as a whole the exercise was successful, but the lack of trained personnel was a handicap and that

1　*The 'attack' on Hastings and St Leonards, 29 January 1938.*

it was evident that many of the volunteer staffs engaged were not up to the desired standard and would require further individual training before any additional outdoor exercise could take place; that the proposed February exercise has therefore been abandoned'.[6]

The apathy felt towards possible war was encouraged by the Hastings branch of the Peace Pledge Union, which met on alternate Fridays at 54 Warrior Square from 1936 until the war proper began. The anti-war group described themselves thus: 'The Hastings Peace Group consists of men and women who: (1) are convinced that war is an avoidable evil, (2) are studying current events and literature in order to strengthen this conviction in their own minds and to equip themselves for more effective peace propaganda'.[7] At the mock attack on Hastings, 30 members of the peace group staged an anti-war demonstration with peace propaganda placards. Among the chief issues of concern they drew attention to was the high price of gasmasks, asserting that many of the town's poor would not be able to afford to protect themselves in the event of war.[8] A Home Office defence report noted that, 'The most prevalent form of British Union propaganda has been the chalking of slogans and the pasting of posters in public places ... the Hastings branch of the Union is publishing a weekly cyclostyled sheet in which it is intended to expose conditions in Hastings'.[9] By the time enemy action had begun to affect the country following the outbreak of war, most anti-war groups, including Hastings', peacefully faded into the background, their main objective having failed.

The subsequent months saw Europe plunge further towards the brink of total war. On 13 March 1938, Germany annexed neighbouring Austria in only a matter of hours. Hitler then aimed his military threats toward

Czechoslovakia. His claim on the country focused upon one area, the Sudetenland, which was mainly inhabited by German-speaking Czechs.[10] During the anxious months of March, April and May, town officials believed that war had become unavoidable and the pace of implementing protection for the town quickened. The Chief Air Raid Warden, Percy Le May, voiced in the *Hastings & St Leonards Observer* that out of a required 520 air raid wardens, only 100 had so far volunteered, and that if more people did not come forward the organisation was in danger of collapse before it had even become operational.[11] It was also stressed that visitors and holidaymakers, upon whom the town relied, needed to feel that Hastings was a safe place to spend time and that it was 'business as usual'. Fortunately over 1,000 locals responded to the plea for A.R.P. volunteers during the Munich Crisis.[12] Prime Minister Chamberlain attended the Munich Conference, ratifying a deal with Hitler and French Premier Edouard Daladier that Britain and France would not object to Hitler annexing the Sudetenland if peace were assured throughout the rest of Europe. It was this display of weakness on the part of Chamberlain and Daladier which would give Hitler the belief that the desire for peace would prevent war. Ironically, by this point the only thing which would be able to assure peace was war.

By the time the committee met again on 26 September 1938, A.R.P. preparations were in full swing. The Chief Constable reported to the committee that a letter had been received from the Home Office stating that the matters of the provision of public shelters, the digging of trenches, the assembly and distribution of gas masks and the further construction of

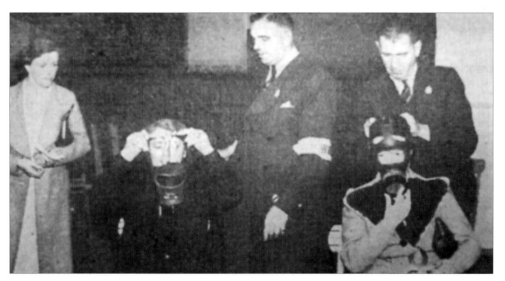

2   *Central Hall, Hastings, September 1938. A.R.P. wardens help fit gasmasks to local residents.*

first aid posts should be dealt with forthwith. Instructions were given for the purchase of 1,000 torches, for use by the air raid wardens, and of six sandbag-filling machines at the cost of £6 each.[13] In addition, 30,000 sandbags were ordered to protect Broomgrove Power Station. Interestingly, the Borough Engineer investigated the possibility of tunnelling into the cliffs for use as air-raid shelters, St Clements Caves evidently being overlooked at this early stage.[14] By October 1938, in collaboration with the Home Office and the General Post Office, the town was equipped with air-raid sirens, which were tested on a monthly basis until the outbreak of war. By 1 October 1938, over 47,000 gasmasks had been distributed in the town to local residents, with thousands more queuing up outside Central Hall to be fitted.[15] The seriousness of the potential for war seemed finally to have been acknowledged.

3   *Hastings Grammar School boys digging trenches at the school, September 1938.*

At Hastings Grammar School, the boys spent the beginning of the Michaelmas term not in lessons but rather digging trenches to be used for air-raid protection and protecting the 'arches' with sandbags.[16] M. Desmond Paine, a pupil at the school, recalls: 'We began by digging trenches on the sacred prefect's lawn and with railway sleepers built shelters. Until the beaches were wired and mined, we had spent many afternoons filling sandbags for the local defences.'[17]

Ken Perkins also remembers returning from the summer holiday ready to enter the fifth year and quite enjoying the trench-digging. Ken remembers that the trenches, dug with pick-axes and shovels, were, rather frustratingly, never actually used as shelters[18] as they were deemed unsuitable by the Borough Engineer. The shelters could, however, be used by the general public if desired.[19]

Six months after the Munich agreement had been ratified, Hitler had violated the treaty and annexed Czechoslovakia. As predicted by Hitler, France and Britain stood by and watched. On 30 March 1939, Chamberlain signed a piece of paper which would be the final catalyst for war when he guaranteed Poland would be defended from the Nazi war machine.

In Hastings security measures were put into position, and plans involving more than 600 voluntary workers were afoot by May 1939, which were enforceable at a moment's notice. Hastings could be instantly readied to receive up to 11,000 children and adults from London in the event of war.[20] The Home Office incorrectly predicted that Hastings would not be an enemy target, as a report shows:

> Hastings has peculiar geographical advantages owing to the hilly character which has prevented close building areas; that it is considered that Hastings is an almost invulnerable area, to which refugees would be sent for safety and that the town would be amongst the last to be provided with [Morrison] steel shelters.[21]

The town's first blackout passed off successfully on Saturday 8 July 1939 as part of a wider test across Sussex and Kent. The public had been asked to extinguish lights from 11 p.m. until 4 a.m., and, with few exceptions, the town fell into the darkness of the county at the allotted time.[22] Despite the great lengths to which the Hastings Corporation and the A.R.P. Committee had gone, the general belief was still that there would be no war. The holidaymakers flocked to the town in their customary droves during the summer months, undeterred by the looming crisis and determined not to let Hitler spoil their break. The *Hastings & St Leonards Observer* found the view on the streets to be rather optimistic: '"There will be no war" is the view one hears confidently on every hand by visitors and residents alike.' Paradoxically, this quote fell under the ominous headline of 'Crisis activity behind the scenes'. The illuminations along the seafront and in Alexandra Park had been extinguished at night since 24 August along with a reduction in street lighting throughout the town. Rather comically, but the subject of much complaint and criticism, both piers were still heavily illuminated.[23]

4 *Ken Perkins, May 1945.*

Had enemy aircraft crossed the Channel at this time they could not have had a better indication of a hidden population! Although the prospect of war was easily, and often intentionally, ignored, hints of a military build-up began to appear. Olga Walker reveals the mixed feelings felt in Hastings at this time:

> The summer holidays of 1939 are remembered as relaxed and jolly, with our tent on the beach watching Biddy the Tubman [a popular Hastings entertainer]. In August I went to Girl Guide camp for two weeks, at Lyndhurst in the New Forest, but this was cut short, our Guiders were worried by the imminent threat of war and the sight of tanks on the open road, heading towards the coast. We had travelled by train and at some point on the return trip we passed an aerodrome where the pilots were already sitting in their planes, this shook us and made us realise how near to war we were.[24]

On 1 September 1939, despite the upbeat atmosphere in Hastings, the inevitable outbreak of war was signalled when Hitler's armies marched into Poland, quickly taking control of the country. Just before 11.30 a.m. the same day, the first influx of 300 evacuees arrived at Hastings train station. Suddenly the town had turned from the sedate, seaside resort of prior years to a bustling town with a grave task to perform. Buses and trains loaded with schoolchildren, unsure of their new surroundings, some of them never having even seen the sea before, arrived in Hastings.[25] For many of the evacuees, some as young as five years old, it was their first time away from home. Stepping from the train into the seaside town, with only teachers and classmates familiar to them, many of the children were deeply unhappy at being torn apart from their families in such a way. The new arrivals, numbering nearly 3,000, were greeted by volunteers keen to help the Londoners settle into their new environment as quickly and comfortably as possible. Marjory Manton had been working for the W.V.S. and helped to deal with the trainloads of school children arriving from London. She found that many of them were far from adequately clothed. Fortunately her husband worked for Marks and Spencer in Hastings at the time and so they were able, out of their own funds, to purchase more clothing for

5   *Olga Walker and her brother, 1939.*

some of the children.[26] Brenda Wallis recalls her father and boyfriend's involvement in the reception of the evacuees, a result of their membership of the Boys Brigade: 'My father, boyfriend [later husband] and other members of the Boys Brigade and Scouts went down to the White Rock Baths where there was a clearance place, and they helped them carry their luggage to wherever they were going to be billeted.'[27]

Eleven-year-old schoolboy Dennis Layell was one of the children evacuated from Greenwich to Hastings on 1 September and remembers the day's events clearly:

6 *Dennis Layell aged 11.*

> We assembled at school at 8 a.m. with our gasmasks, labels and me with a rucksack. We then went by train to New Cross station and travelled to Hastings. I didn't know where we were going or for how long. I thought it an adventure, not worried about it at all. Some boys who had not been away from home, or from parents were a bit apprehensive. It was a corridor train, so we could move about a bit, and we had our own teachers with us. We ate lunch on the train, arriving in the early afternoon. From Hastings station we were moved to Sandown School. After a short wait, another boy and myself were taken to our billet. They were expecting two girls, but we were a boys school.[28]

Also among the evacuees from Greenwich, nine-year-old Patricia Pockett arrived with her six-year-old sister and recalls: 'On arrival in Hastings I do remember the chocolate we were given. We stayed with a family in Alfred Street who treated us well. My sister cried herself to sleep on the first night away, though.'[29]

That evening, as a further protection for the capital, 350 patients were removed from London hospitals and were shared among the town's three main hospitals: the Royal East Sussex, the Buchanan and the Municipal Hospital.[30]

From day one the evacuees received a mixed reaction from local residents. Although most were accommodating and welcoming of the new arrivals, feeling sympathy for their plight, others found some of the evacuees to be less than desirable. Derek Marsh recalls his mother taking in two brothers from London. One of the brothers used to steal regularly from Woolworths and when the police eventually caught up with him they found his room full of items stolen from the shop. The boy ran away, trying to get back to London, but was caught via a trail of raided churches throughout the countryside.[31] The local paper ran several horror stories about a minority of unruly children, with counter-claims by other surrogate parents with well-behaved and polite children.[32] The national Police Duty Room reported to the Home Office that, 'The position everywhere is said to be quiet and the public morale excellent. Generally speaking, evacuation appears to have been carried out without incident at the receiving end, but there have been complaints of evacuees arriving in a verminous condition and suffering from skin diseases.'[33] Hastings, as with many reception towns, struggled to keep the evacuees within its boundaries, as parents recalled their children, dismissing any notions of future conflict; a feeling of complacency had gripped the country. Official reports put the total figure of evacuees returning to London at 40 per cent.[34]

On 3 September 1939 came the news which everybody feared, but to which they had become resigned. At 11.15 a.m. wirelesses across the nation broadcast Prime Minister Neville Chamberlain's solemn news to a quiet, expectant country: Hitler had not replied to the ultimatum to withdraw his troops from Poland, and therefore a state of war existed between Germany and England. Reaction to the news was varied across the town as people sat by their wirelesses uncertain of what the future would bring. Some, with experience of the Great War, were filled with a deep concern and sadness for what lay ahead. Many people were in church at the time and several ministers did not know what to do with their assembled parishioners. In the confusion of the morning, many churches sent the assembled congregation home, though what they thought this would achieve, other than instilling fear into them, is difficult to imagine. Brenda Glazier was attending Sunday school at the Calvert Methodist Church and, with the rest of the Sunday school, was told to go home: 'I rushed home up the hill and I ran indoors and said, "Mummy, I've got to put my gasmask on because there is now war", and I was very scared. I needed an awful lot of comforting.'[35]

Ken Jones remembers being in church when the announcement of war came: 'I was a choirboy in Emmanuel Church on the West Hill. The churchwarden came and whispered a few words to the vicar, who said, "We are now at war with Germany, I think the choirboys had best go home!"'[36] Evidently the news caused severe panic and confusion among the congregation, with many people believing they risked being bombed before they could even reach their own front doors. Terry Breeds was also in Emmanuel Church choir that day and remembers: 'The day that war broke out I was singing in the choir when the vicar, Jason Battersby, announced the news, and everyone went home thinking that an air raid was imminent.'[37] Les Breach was 10 years old and living with his family at Croft Road when the announcement of war came through. He recalls the time clearly:

I was at home with my mother and sister (aged three) and we listened to Neville Chamberlain's broadcast informing us that the nation was at war. Mum was very upset and cried a little. Much to my (later) shame, I felt somewhat excited, not really understanding the dreadful reality. My sister was naturally quite unmoved, but, as was felt before, it would surely be all over by Christmas.[38]

For Olga Walker, her family's reaction to the news was more pragmatic and resigned: 'In late August an elderly aunt and her companion came to live with us. We listened to the Prime Minister's speech on the wireless, and at the end Auntie Cissie insisted that we all needed a drop of brandy: this included my brother and me.' For Eveline Edwards, the news came at a rather inopportune time:

War broke out the day after my 15th birthday and that year everybody forgot my birthday because they were all thinking about the war coming. I was at home with my mum and dad and listened to the news coming on the radio. I can see my mum now sitting on the arm of the chair and my dad in his chair. Everyone knew it was coming, but to hear Chamberlain announce it, we knew it was happening.

The news had little time to be absorbed before, minutes later, the first air-raid alert sounded across the country, triggered by an unidentified aeroplane entering British airspace. Many knew that it was unlikely to be a bombing raid so soon, but others reacted with bewilderment, and some of the volunteer sector sprang into action. Ken Perkins was working as a Scout messenger volunteer for the A.R.P. at the time and recalls rushing to the headquarters in Queen's Road after the air-raid siren sounded, fearing he would be needed.[39] In the event it turned out to be a French aircraft which did not have a flight plan logged. Despite being a false alarm, the incident left many people feeling jittery.[40]

After the initial panic following the declaration of war, the town began to get back to its old routines and life went on as normally as possible under the circumstances, although even minor changes such as the blackout greatly affected the town. Each week the local paper printed a list of the coming week's blackout times, which the police and A.R.P. wardens would strictly uphold, patrolling the streets and taking their duties very seriously. They could often be heard shouting into lit windows, 'Put that light out!' Many disobeyed the blackout and were shamed by having their names printed in the local paper, as well as being fined 10s. under the lighting restrictions order for showing light which might aid enemy aircraft to bomb the town. Among those fined was, rather ominously, Ernest Gummerson[41] of the *Swan Hotel* in the High Street, who would later lose three of his family in one of the worst bombing raids on the town. The blackout's imposition saw the number of deaths and accidents directly attributable to the lack of lighting rise dramatically. Several

elderly people were reported to have fallen down pitch-black staircases, and the number of car accidents and people being knocked down by cars rose dramatically. The number of road deaths in Britain rose to 1,155 in December 1939, an increase of 212 on the previous year. Of those, 895 had occurred at night.[42] Joan Rider recalls a close call one dark night caused by the lighting restrictions enforced upon vehicles:

> Cars had to travel on side lights with strips across to dim them. My mother refused to travel in a car during the dark hours, declaring it was unsafe to do so. One night, as we travelled back to Brede, crossing a narrow bridge, suddenly in the darkness an army vehicle travelling at speed caused my father to swerve and hit the bridge.

7 *Joan Rider, 1943.*

Fortunately, both Joan and her father escaped unhurt. Joan adds: 'My father said we shall always be reminded of the incident as long as the bridge stands. So it was until the bridge was widened years later.'[43]

Despite all the new regulations which were imposed on the town, people largely went about business as usual, while supporting the war effort wherever possible. At Christmas, Hastonians responded nobly when requested to help entertain the evacuee children, with various lectures, comedy sketches and dances being performed to distract them from memories of home at such a family-orientated time of the year.[44] Dennis Layell has the memory of all the evacuees filling the White Rock Theatre to watch a performance of Hansel and Gretel, and of being entertained by the Winkle Club who visited the school.[45] All in all, Christmas 1939 was a relatively quiet one, although the town would quickly become unrecognisable during the coming weeks and months.

Two

EVACUATION, THE BATTLE OF BRITAIN AND THE FIRST RAIDS, 1940

So far the war had only required a few minor adjustments on the part of Hastings residents in the form of the blackout and the reception of evacuees. However, just four months into the war it had become necessary to adapt to drastic changes in meal-times because rationing came into force throughout the country. From 8 January 1940, customers were limited as to how much bacon, butter and sugar they could purchase from their local shops. Other items which were added to the list in 1940 due to their scarcity were tea, cream, meat and petrol. Other items were added in subsequent years as they too became harder to obtain.

In early 1940 fears began to spread through the town regarding the number of 'enemy aliens' who were able to roam freely, with the possibility that they may be spies.[1]

During the period of the 'Phoney War' (so called due to the relative lack of impact compared to what followed later) aliens were initially free to carry on as they had before. Many families of German or Italian origin who had lived in the town for several years were suddenly being persecuted for crimes committed by their home countries. A similar feeling was felt throughout the country, as reported by a Home Office report which stated that, 'Anxiety is expressed in some parts of the country at the presence of uninterned alien enemies.'[2] Even German Jews were not spared some locals' contempt. A Mr Russell wrote in the *Hastings & St Leonards Observer*, 'These alien Jews are Germans and in their hearts loyal to their country, not to England.'[3] The number of enemy aliens who were working as spies for their country is not known, but that they existed in the town is known. Royal Navy Lieutenant Geoffrey Price experienced an enemy spy first-hand in Hastings:

> It was my father's regular habit to meet with his old friends every morning in the local coffee house and I duly joined them. There was a newcomer with the regulars who was introduced to me as a Lieutenant-Commander in the Royal Navy and he informed me that he, too, was on leave and had been in command of a submarine, H.M.S. *Sunfish*, which had been sunk during

the Norwegian campaign ... I had no reason to doubt him and he seemed
a pleasant sort of chap and rather typical of the regular Navy. However, after
meeting him over coffee on a few occasions I thought that he was not very
knowledgeable about naval ships so I went along to the Municipal Library
and looked him up on the Navy List. No such person featured there so my
next call was on the police. Further information was sought from the Navy
which also drew a blank and I was asked to get a bit closer to him and his
friends. This I did and found that he was friendly with a German family
who had been settled in Hastings for a number of years. The father of the
family was a freelance photographer making postcards of the towns and
beauty spots all along the coast ... My 'spy' proved to be an ex-merchant
seaman who was supplying information to the enemy. He was lucky only to
get a long prison sentence.[4]

It was perhaps the presence of spies in the town, relaying such crucial
information as the fact that the town's hotels were full to bursting with
soldiers, that would cause Hastings to suffer such heavy bombing. In June,
Reginald George William Newell, who was holidaying in Hastings, was arrested
on the Fire Hills for having in his possession a notebook containing detailed
information and maps of things deemed to be of national importance
in Sussex. He had been spotted by a policeman writing a letter, which
was later revealed to contain detailed information regarding the blackout,
rationing, signposts and evacuation.[5] Whether the man had been planning
to send the information to the enemy, or, as he attested, to his mother, is
not known, though quite what his mother wanted with such information
is another question.

BLACKOUT TIMES

Week commencing January 13th

	Begins	Ends
Saturday	4.43 p.m.	7.32 a.m.
Sunday	4.45 p.m.	7.31 a.m.
Monday	4.46 p.m.	7.31 a.m.
Tuesday	4.48 p.m.	7.30 a.m.
Wednesday	4.49 p.m.	7.29 a.m.
Thursday	4.51 p.m.	7.25 a.m.
Friday	4.53 p.m.	7.27 a.m.

Blackout times 13 January 1940.

CURFEW

Week commencing July 13th

	Begins	Ends
Today (Saturday)	9.44 p.m.	4.28 a.m.
Sunday	9.42 p.m.	4.29 a.m.
Monday	9.41 p.m.	4.30 a.m.
Tuesday	9.40 p.m.	4.31 a.m.
Wednesday	9.39 p.m.	4.32 a.m.
Thursday	9.38 p.m.	4.33 a.m.
Friday	9.37 p.m.	4.34 a.m.

The first week's curfew times.

On 10 May 1940, Winston Churchill became Prime Minister after Neville Chamberlain lost a vote of confidence over his ineffectual handling of the war so far and the tardiness with which he had dealt with the political situation. Churchill was quick to rectify the situation, and the pace of developments in the town was astounding. Coinciding with the fall of France, Holland and Belgium, the Home Office took the decision that all enemy aliens should be captured and on 12 May 1940 they were rounded up by Hastings Police, who made a rapid sweep of the town, interning all persons of German or Austrian nationality for the duration of the war.[6] Later, aliens of other nationalities were ordered 20 miles inland.[7] Suddenly the reality of the war hit home; the enemy was only held back by little over 20 miles of water, and public attitudes towards other nationalities and anti-war organisations hardened considerably.[8] The real possibility of invasion permeated for the first time the town's thoughts, although, as a Home Office report suggested, 'The possibility of an invasion is faced in a calm and confident spirit'.[9]

On Tuesday 14 May 1940, Anthony Eden made a radio appeal for people to join the Local Defence Volunteers, designed to tackle any enemy landing in the town, particularly by parachute. Eight hundred local men, mostly veterans from the last war, volunteered, the first man arriving at Hastings Police Station before the broadcast had even ended.[10] These volunteers would later become the Home Guard, and were issued with uniforms and whatever weapons, often antiquities from the last war, could be mustered. It is not without reason that the Home Guard are

8   *Edwin Barnes, 1942.*

often portrayed armed with broom handles and other such ineffectual weaponry. These men worked hard for the town, ensuring that vital defences were maintained, and would have played a pivotal role in the town's defence in the event of an invasion. The effect these men had on morale should not be underestimated. Brenda Wallis' father, Edwin Barnes, was among the first men in Hastings to volunteer as a Local Defence Volunteer:

He was one of the ones who went there straight away as he'd done service in the previous war. He very quickly became a sergeant. They did their duty every fourth night and I can remember his rifle being stood up in the corner of the bedroom, and I can remember him cleaning it and getting it ready. The Headquarters was in Sedlescombe Road South in a large empty house, and they went there, and then went out to patrol the town, sometimes Hollington and Silverhill, sometimes as far as the *Bull Inn* on Bexhill Road – that was the end of their patrol. They were on the look-out for parachutists, as we were told that German parachutists might land in the town and they might come disguised, not necessarily in German uniform, some said like nuns or something like that! They were on the lookout for anything suspicious, and making sure everything was in order along the seafront, no fences broken, that kind of thing. My boyfriend did it for a few months before going into the R.A.F. At the time he did it though, they'd just got the armbands with 'L.D.V.' on, they didn't have a uniform or guns for the first few months, and they sort of used anything they could lay their hands on that could be a weapon of some kind. My dad had a rifle very early on, he must have had it in the first issue.[11]

Wednesday 22 May 1940 brought Hastings some interesting visitors from overseas. Two haggard, soaked and coal-dust-covered Belgians arrived in Hastings with several other French and Belgian refugees carrying two suitcases containing 13 million Belgian francs from the Belgian Railway. The two men had escaped Brussels as the enemy marched in and had to leave many records and books pertaining to the railway behind. One of the men, M. Delory, said after the incident:

We left Brussels with a car and three lorries loaded with all the books and records of the railway … For a considerable distance we found the roads were impassable, the enemy was rumoured to be ahead; so we turned back. On the way we passed many dead civilians by the roadside, innocent people who had been machine-gunned by enemy airman. Distracted mothers held up their babies in arms to us as we passed them, but we could do nothing. I found every vessel in the port had left except three small Belgian tugs which had sought refuge there. I found a number of men who wished to leave the port, and with the aid of a party of French soldiers and sailors who kept back hundreds of refugees on the quays who could have swarmed on board the tug, we got safely to sea. I left on the quayside my car and the three lorry loads of books and records, taking only a few personal belongings and the two suitcases crammed with banknotes. Just as we steamed out the town was attacked by enemy aircraft.

The money was later deposited in a bank for the purpose of one day paying the railway workers, although whether this was achieved or not is not known.[12] It is very likely it was this event which was witnessed by Olga Walker:

On the trolley bus going along the seafront and along the Ridge we began to see palls of black smoke rising from across the Channel; we could see them from the High School playground and sometimes wondered if we could hear gunfire. Then we noticed small boats and strange fishing boats coming inshore to the pier and sad looking people with small suitcases being put into buses.

On Monday 26 May began one of the most daring and successful naval rescue operations of the war which came to be known as the 'Miracle of Dunkirk'. Any shallow-draught vessel which was able to get to Dover to take part in the expedition was called upon for assistance. For a bizarre and unknown reason Hitler had ordered the advancing Panzer divisions, which were just short of Dunkirk, to stop in their tracks, giving rise to the possibility of a partial evacuation of Allied troops from the Dunkirk beaches. On Saturday 30 May, 10 Hastings fishing boats, the lifeboat *The Cyril and Lilian Bishop* and the fireboat all joined hundreds of other little boats thronging the channel, and headed to Dover in order to assist the Navy in the evacuation. Iona Muggridge recalls standing on the shore watching them head off and, like many others, guessing at what was taking place but not daring to breathe a word for fear of who might be listening, the wireless later confirming her ideas.[13] In the event, only the lifeboat, which was coxed by George Moon, was used in the evacuation. His niece Carol Boorman recalls that he and the crew were fully prepared and ready to take the boat over to Dunkirk, but were prevented from doing so by the Navy, who commandeered the boat. Upon George's arrival back in the town he got quite upset as locals unfairly called him a coward for not taking the boat over, something which grieved him for a long time afterwards.[14] Apparently, what had caused the lifeboat to be commandeered was the crews of the first three lifeboats to arrive at Dover, those of Hythe, Walmer and Dungeness. Upon learning what was expected of them and their boats, they had refused to make the journey themselves. The Navy ordered them from their boats and sent them home.

When the other lifeboats arrived at Dover, including *The Cyril and Lilian Bishop*, the civilian crew were sent home by train and the boat was taken over by the Navy.[15]

When Hitler realised what was happening at Dunkirk, the Panzers were ordered on to prevent the mass escape, but it was too late: the Allies had mounted a ring of artillery around the stricken soldiers and the evacuation continued until 4 June.[16] Nobody involved with the evacuation could have predicted such a success: 338,226 British, French and Belgian soldiers were safely removed from the beaches of Dunkirk and ferried back to the shores of Dover. When the lifeboat did arrive back in Hastings, it bore significant scarring from its adventures and needed an appeal to the public for donations in order to restore it so that it could continue its vital work throughout the war.[17]

Unfortunately, in order to secure the escape of so many men, it was necessary for a group of men to stay behind, acting as a rear guard until the evacuation was complete and the last of the men safely on his way to Dover. The men left behind were promptly rounded up by the advancing German forces and interned in prisoner-of-war camps. Among the few who were captured was Hastings resident Ronald Parish, who was held prisoner for four years in Germany.

Soon after the Dunkirk evacuations, on 6 June 1940, Prime Minister Winston Churchill gave what would become one of the defining speeches

9   *The battered* Cyril and Lilian Bishop *on arrival in Hastings from Dunkirk.*

of the war to a crowded House of Commons. Churchill had earmarked this day a week previously, believing it would be his difficult job to announce that perhaps only 20-30,000 troops had been saved in what could have been one of the worst defeats in military history. In the end, his speech spelled out the miraculous deliverance that occurred, ending with the now famous words:

> We shall go on to the end, we shall fight in France, we shall fight on the seas and oceans, we fight with growing confidence and growing strength in the air, we shall defend our island, whatever the cost may be, we shall fight on the beaches, we shall fight on the landing grounds, we shall fight in the fields and in the streets, we shall fight in the hills; we shall never surrender.[18]

10   *Ronald Parish, 1942.*

The connotation of Churchill's speech was to prepare the country for possible invasion. Churchill was fully aware that Britain was in no real position to defend itself against invasion – 840 anti-tank guns had been left behind in France, leaving only 167 for home defence, and the majority of field guns were also left at Dunkirk. As David Lampe asserts in his book *The Last Ditch*, the situation was dire indeed: 'Museums all over Britain were being ransacked for serviceable weapons, and among those ordered back into service were 300-year-old howitzers.'[19]

Churchill's speech, so soon after the evacuation of Dunkirk, made life in the town more apprehensive and arduous, removing it even further from the image of the peaceful seaside town of the previous year. Day-to-day life changed constantly as more and more regulations came into force. Church bells were ordered to remain silent, to be used only in the event of enemy parachutists or airborne troops landing in the town. That same week, scrap metal around the town, including the gates to West Marina Gardens, was beginning to be removed to be melted down and used for weapons.[20] Overnight the town suffered the consequences of war further when, on Friday 21 June, it lost its identity with the removal of all signposts, posters, bus signage and so on bearing the town's name – rendering it merely a 'South-East town'. The seriousness of the situation was further compounded when Hastings became part of a strip of land approximately 20 miles wide, extending from the east coast of England through to Portland, known as a Defence Area, which essentially banned all non-residents.[21] Road blocks were installed at all entry points to the town and were strictly guarded by the military. This Defence Area ban all but killed the coming holiday season, dealing the town yet another severe blow. The cut-off point 20 miles inland was in the Uckfield area, where the River Uck was greatly widened and heavily fortified with anti-tank concrete pillars. This was to be a stronghold from which the freedom of the country would be fought for in the event of invasion. The town's beaches very quickly became no-go areas, as they were laced with barbed wire, anti-landing blocks and mines.

The final evidence that Hastings was in grave danger, should any have been necessary, came with the re-evacuation of the London children who had made Hastings their home for nine months. They left the town on Sunday 23 June, on another mystery voyage, bound for 'somewhere in Wales'.[22] This left little doubt as to the government's opinion regarding the safety of Hastings. A secret War Cabinet defence report described the situation thus:

> The scheme for the evacuation of schoolchildren from vulnerable areas has been reviewed in the light of the situation created by the enemy occupation of Holland, Belgium and part of Northern France. It was decided that a number of districts on the East and South East coasts ought no longer to be used as reception areas and that arrangements should be made for the early evacuation of schoolchildren.[23]

It could only be a matter of time until Hastings' own vulnerable were removed to safer areas, as the town entered one of the darkest periods in its history: the 'Phoney War' was about to come to an abrupt end.

Life became tougher still in Hastings when, on 13 July 1940, the government imposed an official curfew on coastal towns throughout the country, including Hastings, to coincide with blackout times. The curfew ruled that no person would be permitted outdoors in the town between half an hour after sunset and half an hour before sunrise, which, for the first day of its introduction, meant that the curfew began at 9.44 p.m. and ended at 4.28 a.m. A comprehensive list of streets covered by the curfew was published in the local paper.[24] On Wednesday 4 September Hastings Magistrates' Court delivered its first prosecution for a resident being in a prohibited area after the 10 p.m. curfew without a permit. Maud Guild was charged under the Defence Regulations with being in East Parade without a permit at 10.40 p.m. the previous evening. She was also charged with being drunk and disorderly at the same time and place. When she was requested to move on she shouted and became hysterical. She was fined £1 for each offence.[25]

11   *Evacuation day – Hastings Grammar School boys waiting at Hastings train station.*

Rather fortuitously, on Sunday 21 July, just five days before the first enemy attack on Hastings, some 3,000 children, representing approximately half the eligible number, were hoarded onto 69 coaches and evacuated to 'safe' reception areas in Hertfordshire and Bedfordshire.[26] All Hastings schools were closed with immediate effect. The Director of Education, Mr W. Norman King, said at the time:

> The Government has decided that Hastings, so far as school children are concerned, is no longer a reception area as it was last September, but an evacuation area … Parents admittedly have a difficult problem, but there can be no question as to their duty to support the Government in this move.[27]

Ken Jones has the memory in June 1940 of the Hastings Grammar School headmaster, Mr M.G.G. Hyder, summoning the whole school to the hall to tell them that the Germans could invade and land in the town at any moment. If that happened, and it were at all possible, pupils should come to school as usual. Ken recalls, 'He also said that we were all to be on our best behaviour, as it was a very anxious time for our parents. He then told us that in a month's time the school was to be evacuated to St Albans.'[28]

12   *St Albans train station after disembarkation.*

Parents were expressly asked not to attend the railway station with their children on the day of evacuation, in view of the congestion which would be caused, something almost unilaterally ignored. The children were each given a postcard so that upon arrival at the unknown destination they could write home immediately and inform parents of their new temporary address.[29] In the end 280 boys took the train to St Albans.[30] Another Hastings Grammar School pupil, M. Desmond Paine, recalls the time of evacuation:

> We were given 48 hours' notice to report to the station with one suitcase and NO extra items. We were there at 7.30 a.m. with parents and siblings wearing luggage with our names and school on them and a huge variety of 'extras' including bicycles, cricket bats, footballs and telescopes! There was another complete school also in the melée. Some hours later we were sorted out and loaded, and the train slowly moved off, but only as far as St Leonards where another school went through the same confusion. From there the journey was stop and go. At St Albans we got off with the now familiar platform preliminaries. At a local school reception centre we were given a chocolate bar and taken off in groups to be billeted. Some places put up great resistance to taking evacuees and I was told to wait in the hall until the escort fetched a policeman to enforce the order![31]

After only one and a half weeks of the schools being evacuated to various reception areas, a disagreement began in the pages of the *Hastings & St Leonards Observer* which would continue for the duration of the war, regarding whether or not the schools in the town should remain open for those children who, for whatever reason, had not been evacuated. A letter from 'A Mother' states, 'We have confidence in our Government. There is evidently some reason for this evacuation. Do people remember what happened to the children in France and elsewhere? It is up to the parents to co-operate and give the children that little extra safety.'[32] A letter published in the local paper on 17 August from 'An Evacuee' was a great lift to those parents uncertain as to whether they had taken the right action by sending their children away to the reception areas:

> Sir, on behalf of the Hastings evacuees, especially the Hastings Grammar School boys, I would like to tell everybody how happy we all are. Our fears when we left Hastings were soon put out of our minds when we found out what jolly, sporty people we had come to ... We are all very happy and content, and we shall stay here until the enemy have been defeated, and then we shall come back to good, old Hastings.[33]

Experiences varied greatly with regard to evacuation, but many people had a pleasant experience, making firm, life-long friendships or remaining in the evacuation area long after the war's end. Gordon Dengate describes his positive experience as follows:

13   *Waiting at St Albans bus station.*

14   *Gordon Dengate.*

I was evacuated with Hastings Central School to a lady and gentleman's house called Mr and Mrs Legg and they were really good. I remember her trying to teach me to talk properly and make me sound my vowels in the right way. Eventually she gave up and told my father she presumed it's the way we talk in Hastings! There were occasions they would borrow a bicycle for me and we'd all cycle over to Ware to visit my sister Maisie. Being taken away from home like that, I don't ever remember being upset; life seemed quite interesting, quite an experience.[34]

Twenty-five-year-old Peggy Smith's husband, Tom Smith, was one of the school masters at Christ Church School who in 1940 had to evacuate with the school to Lower Dean in Bedfordshire. Peggy herself was forced to remain in Hastings for a short time whilst she organised the storage of the couple's furniture from their London Road home before joining her husband in Lower Dean. She recalls the evacuation process going quite smoothly and most children enjoying the quiet village life.[35] For Christ Church School pupil Lew Boorman, life was quite happy in Lower Dean, despite there being no electricity or running water in the house in which he was billeted. The evacuation also benefited his father, who used to go around all the Hastings off-licences and buy up their whiskey, which was fairly easy to obtain in Hastings for about 10-15 shillings per bottle, then, when paying a visit to his son, sell it on to the Americans stationed in Bedfordshire who were willing to pay three or four pounds a bottle.[36] Another Christ Church School pupil, Ronald Ollington, reveals how the evacuees were given jobs to do during holiday periods to distract them from thoughts of home: 'During the summer time we helped on the local farms, for which we got extra rations, and any money earned went into the school fund to take us on outings.'[37]

Another Hastings schoolboy to evacuate in July 1940, who also enjoyed his time as an evacuee, was Terry Breeds. He definitely landed on his feet in his first billet:

I was evacuated with the Mount Pleasant Junior School having already taken the entry examination for the Hastings Grammar School. We were sent by train to a beautiful little village near Stevenage, called Walkern. I remember waiting in the school assembly room to be allocated, and four of us went with a Major and Mrs Squarey, who owned the largest Georgian house in the village: It was the Old Rectory. It stood in its own grounds and they owned a mile of the River Lee with rowing boat and a raft. We used to get a set of bows and arrows from the gym and go out 'water-ratting' at 5 or 6 a.m. before going to school. They had three horses, tennis court, gymnasium, and servants to wait on us! Two weeks after we had settled in, there was a coach trip laid on for the parents to visit us and when my mother asked if I wanted to go home my reply was 'not likely'! Playing cricket in the school grounds at Walkern cost me two front teeth. I was watching a dog-fight when one of the German planes jettisoned its load. The next

15 *Terry Breeds proudly wearing his new Hastings Grammar School uniform in St Albans.*

thing I knew I was under the desk in school with blood coming out of my mouth. My stay at Walkern lasted until October when I was transferred to St Albans with the Hastings Grammar School. This was a lovely town, but the accommodation this time was in a council house, and a big come-down. I had two further lodgings in St Albans – one with a dental mechanic and his wife (there were always impressions of teeth laying around) and the last was with a lady whose husband was in the services. I must admit that I enjoyed evacuation.[38]

Ware in Hertfordshire received 188 girls from Hastings High School. The evacuation was organised by the headmistress, Miss F.M. Cummin. Upon arrival in Ware, the girls were taken to Ware Grammar and Central Schools.[39] For Olga Walker, the day of evacuation, which began at 11 a.m. is still incredibly vivid:

We were checked into forms and put into coaches: for us a big adventure, heartbreak for our parents. They had no idea where we were bound or when they would see us again, each child was required to bring a small suitcase with a change of clothing and a packet of sandwiches to see us through the day. At Hastings Station we got into trains and off we set. Some of us had been to London by train and recognised stations on the line, and then we were going through dense areas of houses which we

16   *Maisie Pocock.*

decided must be London. This changed again to open country and eventually the train stopped at a station which only had one platform, most unusual from our point of view. We all piled out and were formed into a crocodile, each with our suitcase, and started to walk through the streets of this unknown town. It was probably a 15-minute walk and we arrived at a school. There we were handed out to people who had offered or been coerced into taking in these children from 'The South Coast'. My particular friend, Dulcie, and I were walked up the street with one of the organisers and handed over to a couple whose name I have forgotten. For many of us it was the first time we had experienced gas lamps, outside lavatories and no bathroom; washing at the sink whilst breakfast was being cooked around one eventually became accepted but not enjoyed. For a time, bathing was arranged at the Allen and Hanbury Sports Club, but when that was commandeered by the Army, that ended that. Dulcie and I had been told when we were introduced to our foster parents that it was only a temporary stay, as we were not wanted. Our foster father was very kind, he was the head fireman of Ware, in Hertfordshire, and took us out with him on his duty tours.[40]

Maisie Pocock was evacuated for 12 months with the High School and billeted with Mrs Armstrong and her family, and remembers settling in well with them, a process made easier when her cousin Eileen later joined the billet. Whilst being evacuated, Maisie received the news of another cousin's death in Hastings, the bad tidings sent in a black-edged envelope indicating that there had been a death.[41]

For some children, the time of evacuation was unsettling and unwelcome, as recalled by Charles Clark, who recollects the difficult day of evacuation:

We were evacuated to Welwyn Garden City and the thing that sticks in my mind is the tearful farewells as we were put onto the trains at Hastings Railway Station, with our small cases of luggage, gas masks, and the label on the lapels of our coats saying who we were. I had to look after my younger sister, with parental instructions not to be separated, which after arrival at Welwyn Garden City did not work very well as the foster parents did not want a brother and sister. The period of evacuation was the unhappiest time of my life.[42]

For Joan Fincham, too, the unsettled period of evacuation was an unhappy time:

> I was an only child just seven years old when I was sent, with another girl whom I did not know, to a large house in Harpenden, Hertfordshire. It was a most unhappy time for me and I was moved on from one place to another until eventually my mother came up from Hastings to join me.[43]

To others, evacuation was simply harrowing and traumatic. Brenda Glazier recalls waiting at Hastings train station to be evacuated:

> I can always remember my mother coming to see us off at the station and we had these gas masks around our necks, carrying our suitcases with our bits and pieces. I can see their faces now as they watched me go. I was only there eight months, I wouldn't have lasted longer than that. I was evacuated with my cousin who was older than me, but she only stayed with me for one week, she was so homesick that she went home and I was left there very, very homesick indeed. One day I remember vividly, I was coming home from school in St Albans and I saw my father coming towards me and I ran into his arms and said, 'Daddy, daddy, please take me home, daddy.' And he said, 'I can't, darling.' I told him to tell my mum that I'd stopped sucking my thumb. In my childish thoughts, I associated that I had been sent away because I had done something wrong. Within a few days of that, the people that I was living with told me that my mother was coming to collect me on the following Sunday, so I came home.[44]

Under the heading 'Children without Schools – A Grave Local Problem', 'Flotsam and Jetsam' remarked in the local paper that the number of children who remained in Hastings ranged from hundreds to thousands in number, children who 'will have to help rebuild the post-war world and play their part in the life of post-war Hastings, who are, and have been, receiving no education'.[45] One Hastings boy, Les Breach, recalls, 'I didn't go to school for a couple of years, a fact that I found not to be the least upsetting! Dad made me a wooden Tommy gun and I spent hours at the top of the house shooting at (and destroying!) many German planes.'[46]

Five days after the crowded trains of anxious evacuees departed from Hastings train station came the first bombs to be dropped on the town. At around 7.15 a.m. on Friday 26 July 1940, a lone German bomber dropped 11 H.E. bombs on the West Hill and Cricket Ground areas of Hastings,[47] killing one, seriously injuring two and causing further injury to seven others. This first attack included houses in Gladstone Terrace, Whitefriars Road, Bembrook Road and Priory Road. It damaged six houses so badly that demolition was necessary, with four further houses needing to be evacuated and 48 suffering superficial damage, such as smashed windows and damaged roofs.[48] One of the bombs exploded in front of 10 and 11 Gladstone Terrace, bringing the fronts of the two houses down along with

17   *Gladstone Terrace, 26 July 1940.*

18   *Gladstone Terrace, 2004.*

number 22 opposite. Beryl Latimer (née Stevenson) was asleep in number 10 Gladstone Terrace when the bomb exploded, and recalls:

> My father had left for work at the Gas Works in Bulverhythe and my mother was in the kitchen cleaning the fire grate. My sister Hazel and I were still in bed, fortunately sharing a back bedroom. The bomb exploded at the front of the building, exposing the back rooms, so we were left with our bed sloping towards the front and had a problem getting out of it. Mother was buried under the bricks from the chimney breast. The Civil Defence arrived and took at least a couple of hours to get her out, and when they did, she was badly shocked and covered in soot. She spent a few days in Hospital with some injuries, and it took some days to remove the soot from her body and hair. The most vivid memory I have in looking back at the ruins, is that my father had hung his trousers over the foot of the iron bedstead and they were still there, although the bed stood drunkenly on the half collapsed floor. We were then asked to spend the rest of the day in the church hall in Vicarage Road, West Hill, while accommodation was found for us. All that was left of our previous home was a sideboard and some bits and pieces.[49]

Fortunately, Beryl's 11-year-old sister Brenda had been evacuated to St Albans and was told of the bombing via her teachers at Priory Park School.[50]

The first bombing raids on the town also brought the first of many deaths when Violet Gladys Gooday was killed at her parents' home at 139 Priory Road. The 34-year-old had been a schoolteacher at St Andrew's School and, by a cruel twist of fate, she and her husband Robert had moved only days before she died to her parents' house in Priory Road from their home in Park Drive, which remained unscathed throughout the war.[51] Among the injured in the attack was Alice Millicent Rummery of 17 Lennox Street, Halton who, despite surviving the incident for some time, died of her severe injuries exactly six months later at the Royal East Sussex Hospital.

Why Hastings was subject to these indiscriminate bombing and machine-gunning attacks by enemy aircraft has been the subject of much debate. It is likely, however, that no single reason exists for them; that it is a conglomeration of a variety of reasons. As is suggested in the previous chapter,

19 *The first war dead: Violet Gooday's grave in Hastings Cemetery.*

hundreds of troops were stationed there, which was likely to have been known by the enemy. Added to this, Hastings was an easy target, especially during the preliminary stages when the town was undefended against attack. It is also proposed that pilots used Hastings as a training ground before moving on to the tougher target of the capital. There can also be no doubt that the desire to affect morale was also high on the agenda.

After public concerns over the first wave of bombing in Hastings, the Mayor, Councillor E.M. Ford, launched an Air Raid Distress Fund to give Hastings residents immediate financial assistance after suffering damage from enemy action. Residents were urged by the local paper to hand donations in to the Town Hall at Summerfields. A special service and collection, conducted by the Reverend Jason Battersby and attended by the Mayor, was held at Emmanuel Church for those victims of air raids. In less than two years the Reverend Battersby would himself suffer the loss of his infant daughter in an air raid.[52]

For those left in Hastings the duration of August to October 1940 bore witness to the constant and often dangerous dog-fighting overhead between the R.A.F. and the Luftwaffe, in what came to be known as the Battle of Britain. The skies over Kent and Sussex were filled with battling aircraft, as the Luftwaffe struggled to gain air superiority over the R.A.F. in preparation for Hitler's plan to invade England, code-named Operation Sea Lion. Hitler originally ordered that a landing operation be accomplished in the form of a surprise crossing on a broad front from Ramsgate to an area as far west as the Isle of Wight, thereby incorporating Hastings, to take place in July or August of 1940. Before any such attack could take place, however, certain conditions had to be met. The substantial power of the R.A.F. had to be minimised, so as to preclude any overwhelming resistance to the crossing. The sea routes needed to be cleared of mines and then relaid to prevent a counter-attack by the Royal Navy. It was for these reasons, and because the High Command of the German Army and Navy were at loggerheads over the breadth of the landing, that Hitler continually delayed his final decision over Operation Sea Lion. The allies were in no doubt about Hitler's intention, as a secret document of autumn 1940 reveals:

> It is known that the Germans have approximately two million men under arms, a superior number of aircraft, but inferior naval forces. It is also known that their economic situation compels them to make every endeavour to defeat this country before this coming winter. It is, therefore, generally believed that they will attempt to invade this country in the near future by a combination of airborne and seaborne attack.

A detailed response was drawn up by the R.A.F., the Navy and the Army in order to counter any such invasion.[53] The final draft of Operation Sea Lion was to have four complete divisions of the German 16th Army embark from Rotterdam, Antwerp, Ostend, Dunkirk and Calais, landing between Folkestone and St Leonards, while elements of two divisions of the 9th Army were to leave Boulogne and the Canche Estuary to land between Bexhill and Eastbourne.[54] Should the attack have taken place, the consequences for the town would have been unimaginable. Never before had Hastings residents been so appreciative of and grateful for the intervening Channel. Locally, a secret plan, which was not revealed until the war had ended, was put into effect. Three large Martello tower-style concrete vats were installed along the Hastings coastline, which would, in the event of invasion, have sent a terrifying wave of fire into the sea, fed by oil pumped down huge steel pipes from the camouflaged concrete vats, which would have burnt many enemy invaders alive. The three vats, situated at White Rock Gardens, the Fishmarket and Rock-a-Nore, were decommissioned in June 1945.[55]

Another secret form of defence which was one of Sussex's best kept, wartime secrets was the formation, in May 1940, of the Auxiliary Units – otherwise known as the 'British Resistance'. These were small units of men, mainly farm labourers, who built secret chambers and tunnels in the deepest Sussex countryside, which housed water, food, explosives, grenades, weapons and intelligence-gathering materials. They were designed to spring into action upon the coast being invaded, when the men would take on a sabotage, sniping and intelligence-gathering role, supplying the Home Forces with information from what effectively would have been behind enemy lines. The men who undertook this role did so in the knowledge that their life expectancy would be short. One underground hideout was located at Beauport Park in Hastings.[56]

As the Battle of Britain continued to rage overhead, many locals' experiences moved from safe observation to being accidentally caught in the crossfire of the battling aircraft. Often, however, enemy attacks were of a more deliberate and vicious nature, as people found themselves being fired upon indiscriminately in the streets. One Old Town resident, Iona Muggridge, describes her experiences during this time:

> I think the worst part of the war for me was the first part of it, the Battle of Britain. They used to fire at you in the streets and you dived anywhere, anybody's door you jumped in, otherwise you would get the lot in your back. A lady and I were walking along the pavement and this Jerry plane came over just above the roof-tops and he was firing, and I pushed this lady flying and I jumped behind her, and she said, 'What did you do that for?' I said, 'Well look at that lot,' and you could see the shells going along the pavement and I said, 'You don't want that lot in your back surely?' I know one of them followed my father; he was going back to work and he got into this telephone box near our house and he had to stay in the phone box because this plane went around and around firing at him, and he had to stay there. He phoned work and said he didn't know how long he would be as he was in a phone box and daren't come out.[57]

20 *Iona Muggridge.*

Lew Boorman remembers a near encounter during one Battle of Britain fight:

My most vivid recollection of the war was when I lived in St Joseph's flats, on the corner of Union Street and Alfred Street, which had a flat roof. I was up there on my own at that time, engrossed in watching this dog-fight from the roof between a Messerschmitt and a Spitfire and my mother called me down. As I reached the bottom of the staircase a shower of bullets came down the staircase behind me. Had it been ten seconds earlier I wouldn't be here now. It was a real close one. They weren't shooting at me, they were shooting at each other and I happened to be coming down the stairs. The police took the bullets away for inspection to see if they were anything new.[58]

In nearby Crowhurst, Margaret Humphrey recalls one dog-fight that took place overhead:

My gran and uncle had a Post Office and the chap opposite had a coal yard where he used to deliver coal from by horse and cart. This particular day, we had a dog-fight going on low overhead and of course the horse was harnessed up to the cart ready to go for a delivery and it just bolted up the road, with poor old Mr Goodsell running after it. It was quite funny for us, but it wasn't funny for him. Later the Spitfire came over doing the Victory Roll, so evidently he had got it.[59]

A three-week lull after the initial bombings was shattered at 3.50 p.m. on Wednesday 14 August when a lone bomber dropped six H.E. bombs on Bexleigh Avenue, Pine Avenue and West St Leonards,[60] killing two people: Caroline Frances Felton, of 42 Bexleigh Avenue, who was injured at home but died that day at the Buchanan Hospital from her injuries, and James Thomas Harmer, of 40 Bexleigh Avenue. The attack left one person seriously injured and another slightly injured.[61]

The following day Maggie May Wright was killed at home in Harley Shute Road when a number of German planes left their formation of between 40 and 50 planes, dropping 10 H.E. bombs in the Harley Shute, Maze Hill and Saxon Street areas at 6.58 p.m. Despite much damage to houses and the Masonic Hall, only Maggie May Wright was killed and two more people injured, one of them seriously.[62]

Although at this stage of the war Hastings was unprotected by A.A. guns, the coast was patrolled by two Spitfires, often affectionately referred to as 'Girt and Daisy'. As would be expected, the Spitfires would often successfully shoot down the enemy aircraft they engaged. If successful, they would sometimes emphasise their triumph by performing a 'victory roll' for delighted onlookers. One such successful engagement occurred at 3.38 p.m. on 5 September, when a Messerschmitt 109 flew over Hastings pursued by an R.A.F. Spitfire, attempting to reach the safety of the French coast. It was shot down by the Spitfire and the aircraft ditched into the sea just off Hastings. The German pilot, Fw. Ochenskuhn, bailed out of the stricken plane and took to his dinghy. The Hastings lifeboat was launched and retrieved Ochenskuhn, bringing him ashore for arrest at 5 p.m.[63]

After the initial wave of attacks, which saw the safety of the town deteriorate rapidly, any Hastings residents who wanted to evacuate were encouraged to do so by town officials and were given free transportation to a safer area. On 11 September, six weeks after the first evacuation, the second evacuation of the town, which was more widely heeded, took place. The constant air battles and bombing had frightened over half the town into leaving, many hurrying off to stay with relatives or friends in safer areas of the country. The town's pre-war population of over 65,000 dropped to just 21,000.[64] Frank Gutsell recalls the night before the second evacuation day:

> I remember a loudspeaker coming round the streets telling us we had to be evacuated within the 24 hours. Those of us who didn't have cars, or relatives outside of Hastings, should go by train from Hastings railway station. My mother, sister and I were taken to Yeovil and billeted with a family who didn't make us feel welcome, so we only stayed with them for a month. We returned to Hastings to find the only school which was open was Sacred Heart Convent School. We were taught by nuns and at first only attended school either mornings or afternoons to accommodate all the children.[65]

One family who also evacuated and returned shortly afterwards was the Greenwood family. Eileen Parish recollects her mother asking a soldier what she should do given the threat of invasion. The soldier suggested that they evacuate, as the Germans were sure to invade. So they evacuated to Maidenhead, after having to make the difficult decision, as many people were having to do, as to which of their pets they would keep:

> We had two cats and two dogs at that time and one was picky on food so that wasn't a good policy and she was a bit nervous with the bombs, but the other dog, Heidi, she would eat anything you gave her and was as placid as can be, so we had to have the dog and two cats put down. The trains were packed,

but everybody was okay with the dog. Going through London, she saw the barrage balloons and she barked at them, but dropping bombs or aeroplanes going over and she never turned a hair. So, we evacuated for a fortnight and then returned! My mother wasn't happy being evacuated and when we came back there was nobody here, the place was deserted.[66]

Brenda Wallis, her family and neighbour all decided to take heed of the invasion warning and partook in this voluntary evacuation of the town:

21   *Eileen Parish, 1943.*

These notices went up that evacuation for those that wanted to go was being arranged; women, children and elderly people mainly. My mother, sister and I, and our neighbour, we went together. We had to assemble at Silverhill School which was at the top of Paynton Road and we had to assemble there at 9 a.m., and we were there queuing in twos until 1 o'clock. It was very tedious and we wondered when on earth the buses were going to come for us. They did come at last and took us to Hastings station, and we got onto the train and we had no idea where we were going; it was an 'unknown destination'. There was a German plane which flew over the train whilst we were sitting waiting to pull out of Hastings Station and machine-gunned the train; it was very scary. There wasn't room to get down, but we all sort of cowered and it was all over in a flash. It was a terrible noise, ear-splitting for a few seconds. When we moved off, it must have been about 2.30 p.m. We travelled and travelled, and eventually we disembarked at Glastonbury at about 11.30 p.m., and we were all housed in the local cinema. There were a few mattresses for people who really couldn't manage the seats, and we managed to get a mattress for my grandfather because he was elderly, and they were put up onto the stage area and laid there. We got what sleep we could, but nobody had a very good night's sleep that night. In the morning we were allocated to our billets wherever we were going. I went with our neighbour and we went together to a billet and we actually stayed there for two months. It was a real home from home really, we couldn't fault anything, but we came home after two months when things quietened down a bit here.[67]

In Hastings the bombing continued apace. Clive Vale suffered badly on 12 September when numerous houses in Edmund Road were damaged, later to be classified as 'so badly damaged, demolition necessary'. Number 41 Alfred Road was totally destroyed in the attack, killing its two occupants, Jane Maria Bumstead and 59-year-old William George Dowding.[68] In these attacks, which came at 2.10 p.m., 150 incendiary bombs were dropped on the town, causing less damage than perhaps would have been anticipated given the number used.[69]

The next bombing attack was on Linton Crescent and the Old Town at 2.20 p.m. on Saturday 14 September, and was another instance where the damage done could have been far worse than it in fact was. The attacks on Linton Crescent were undoubtedly aimed at the railway viaduct. Dozens of Hastings' oldest buildings, and

22   *Brenda Wallis, 1942.*

numerous lives, were spared when nine H.E. bombs dropped in a line up All Saints Street, but fortunately failed to explode.[70] As happened fairly frequently in the town, the air-raid siren was sounded after the attacks had taken place, giving people no chance to seek refuge. It was not until 2.58 p.m. that the air-raid siren sounded; the all-clear signal being given at 5.15 p.m. that afternoon. Forty-two minutes later, however, the siren sounded again until 7.19 p.m.[71] That same day a Dornier, attacked by a Spitfire from 602 Squadron, was sent plummeting to the ground from 22,000ft. According to David Rowland, in his book *Spitfires over Sussex*, 'The Spitfire pilot watched but kept his distance, expecting the bomber to explode and break up at any moment. In fact it crash-landed at Eighteen Pounder Farm at Westfield, near Hastings: one crew member bailed out and was never found, while the others were captured.'[72] No record exists of what happened to this missing crew member.

With the high number of Allied aircraft being destroyed in the Battle of Britain, and many more needed as replacements, Alderman Blackman launched the Spitfire Fund in Hastings, promising to donate £1,000 if the town could meet the other £4,000 needed to buy a new Spitfire. Very

23   *The* Hastings *Spitfire.*

quickly the town got behind the Fund and many people began raising and donating money towards it. Within the first week Lord Beaverbrook praised Hastings for raising 40,000 of the necessary 100,000 shillings. Activities included darts players at the *Cambridge Hotel* who scored 'ten or under' being asked to put a halfpenny 'fine' into the Spitfire collection tin, and Mrs F. Rix of 5 and 6 Albert Road giving one shilling to the Fund for every 20s. worth of gold or silver purchased.[73] Collection boxes sprang up all over the town, including at the *Victoria Inn* in Battle Road.[74] Dorothy Wellings remembers an older lady at the St Leonards Parish Church organising a mile of halfpennies along the road for the Fund.[75] In subsequent editions of the local newspaper, much was made of how necessary the Spitfire was to the town and the work the aeroplane did, to the point that no other Allied aircraft would get a mention! As the Battle of Britain raged, sometimes very low overhead, the Spitfire was depicted as a symbol of the country's defiance and resilience against enemy attack. Very often the stories of the 'Victorious Spitfire' shooting down Nazi aircraft into the sea were published in the *Hastings & St Leonards Observer,* perhaps more times than official records would corroborate.[76]

By 21 September the target of £5,000 for the Spitfire Fund had been easily achieved, with the town raising £4,288 plus the gift of £1,000 by Alderman Blackman. The surplus monies were added to the Air Raid Relief Fund.[77] The *Hastings* Spitfire, number R7067, served with several Operational Training Units, mainly with Polish crew, before being taken out of service on 11 August 1944. The exact nature of its demise is not known.

The bombing of the town continued unabated throughout September. On 23 September the air-raid siren sounded four times, yet failed to sound when at 4.15 p.m. a lone raider dropped three H.E. bombs and an oil bomb in the Halton area, rendering many people homeless. Numbers 10-13 Egremont Place, 46-8 and 55-61 Albion Street, and 2-7 South Terrace were all destroyed.[78] A Samaritan report into the incident notes that many other houses were damaged, particularly at the rear. Many residents of the Halton part of Priory Road and Albion Road were taken to The Lindens, a Salvation Army Rest Centre on Upper Maze Hill for air-raid victims. Others were taken to the Municipal Hospital, and some were evacuated or went to relatives because of an unexploded bomb in Priory Road near number 212. Robert and his wife Louisa Annie Winborn both died from the bomb explosion in their home at 46 Albion Street, which took the weight of the blast, and was totally destroyed.[79] Other houses were damaged in Valley Side Road and the top of the High Street.[80] The final air-raid siren of the day began at 9.12 p.m. and, in what must have been a restless night's sleep for the town, finally ended at 5.48 a.m.[81]

Late on Wednesday 25 September an enemy aircraft, a Messerschmitt 110, was spotted on a photo reconnaissance mission over London and was intercepted by Pilot Officer J.M.F. Dewar of 229 Squadron who, after a lengthy chase, put one engine out of action on the enemy aircraft.[82] After a spectacular low-level chase over Hastings, the plane crashed attempting to land at Beaney's Lane on the Ridge.[83] Of the two crew, 24-year-old

24 *The crashed ME110 in Beaney's Lane.*

25   *Eberhard Weyergang and Gustav Nelson's graves, Hastings Cemetery.*

Oberlt. Eberhard Weyergang perished with the aircraft and 27-year-old Fw. Gustav Nelson was thrown clear of the plane.[84] Nelson was captured but died the same day of his injuries. Among the many locals to witness the plane coming down was Jack Hilder, who took parts of it to sell, with the profits going towards the Spitfire Fund at the *Victoria Inn*.[85] Weyergang and Nelson were buried alongside five other German airmen in Hastings Cemetery.[86]

Over the same day and the following, several daylight raids took place on Hastings in Kings Road, Warrior Square, the Gas Holders, Queens Road, Nelson Road, Alfred Street and Carisbrooke Road.[87] In all, 60 H.E. bombs and one oil bomb were dropped, killing five and seriously injuring a further 24 people.[88] Joan Rider remembers being at work in Dengate's furniture shop in Queen's Road when the bomber was circling overhead:

> My father was dictating letters to me and I remember how difficult it was to concentrate, knowing that the pilot was trying to aim for the gasworks at the top of Waterworks Road. One bomb did hit a busy stationer's in Queen's Road near our depository, where Stan Dengate was at the time. Using the phone extension to enquire if he was alright, his reply was, 'I am, but have the girls from Swains with me and one has her clothes ripped off by the blast!'[89]

This was probably part of the raid which was witnessed by Lew Boorman on Alfred Street. 'I was with my father and we looked up and saw this bomb actually dropping from the plane and he dragged me down and bomb went off about 20 yards away, which was a very lucky escape.'[90]

Although many of the raids on Hastings were carried out by lone raiders, on occasion townspeople would look up and see, without prior warning, dozens of enemy aircraft in the skies above them. On 27 September 1940, an A.R.P. warden noted having seen 36 German planes coming in low over the town. Two of these planes, it is noted, were brought down in the sea after a low-flying battle with the R.A.F.[91] According to Martin F. Mace, in his book *They Also Served*, only one of these aircraft was ever found:

> The lifeboat was launched at 5.37 p.m. with the honorary secretary, Commander W. Highfield O.B.E., R.N., going out with her. As she raced her way south through a slight sea, a second report was received stating that a further German plane had crashed in flames six miles further south. On arrival at the location of the first crash, the lifeboat crew came across one survivor, Gefr. J. Feichtmayer, who was badly wounded and, despite having been in the water for two hours, was able to tell the crew of the *Cyril and Lilian Bishop* what had happened. His aircraft, a Junkers Ju-88 bomber had been damaged by R.A.F. fighters whilst trying to bomb London...unable to make France, the German plane ditched in the channel. Oberlt F. Ziel and Fw. F. Niederer had managed to escape the ditched bomber, but both were subsequently found to have drowned ... As for the second burning plane reported to the Hastings lifeboat, no trace was found of her crew.[92]

The A.R.P. logbook of the early hours of Saturday 28 September gives an insightful, somewhat humorous and spirited account of the night's activities, indicating what the town regularly endured:

> 3.15 a.m. – Several bangs in distance. One plane became a nuisance by playing ring o' roses. 3.25 a.m. – More bangs in distance, two nearer. Pilot of plane must be giddy. Wonder if his Mother knows he is out this time of the night. 3.30 a.m. – If a plane travels 500 miles per hour why the heck hasn't he gone. Perhaps he's lost, poor chap.

Later that day the logbook records, '7.55 p.m. – 6 a.m. – O peaceful night! Barry didn't even hear the all clear! Warning lasted 10 hours 5 minutes – Record to date.'[93]

Another report, from the A.R.P. logbook dated 29 September, shows just how much impact the bombings had: 'Loud bang at 4.15 p.m. shook the building. No report from Control – must have been outside the borough.'[94]

At 9.11 a.m. on Monday 30 September, the air-raid siren once again rang out, warning the town of imminent danger. Some, like 17-year-old Hilda Marden, who was in the town centre, ran into nearby shelters; others

26   *The Plaza Cinema. The bomb struck just above the letters PL.*

27   *Site of Plaza Cinema, 2004.*

misguidedly chose to ignore the warning. At 10.30 a.m. came the worst bombing raid the town had seen so far. During an air battle, three H.E. bombs and an oil bomb were dropped, one of which hit the coping of the Plaza Cinema, exploding in mid-air and killing eight people outright, with four others dying later from their injuries. The bomb seriously injured a further 12 people, with 23 suffering minor injuries.[95] Damage to the cinema was described in an official report as including a hole in the roof and 'entrance staircase and doors and ceilings. Canopy and signs, fascia all damaged. All windows throughout. Front of building damaged. Large hole in parapet. Interiors of cinema unexamined'.[96] The four dials of the memorial clock were blown out and many shops in the vicinity sustained

28   *Clifford Arthur Glazier.*

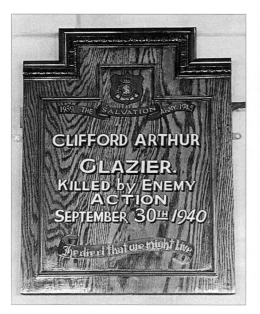

29   *Clifford's memorial in the Salvation Army Citadel; and his grave in the civilian war dead section of Hastings Cemetery.*

30 *George James Brooker.*

damage, including shops and offices in Wellington Place, York Buildings, Cambridge Road, Robertson Street and Braybrooke Road, the houses in which lost all their windows and some ceilings.[97]

Among those who lost their lives was the youngest person to be killed by enemy action to date: 14-year-old Clifford Arthur Glazier, the only child of Jack and Elsie Glazier.[98] Clifford had been waiting in Robertson Street for a bus to take him to a new job in a solicitor's office in Silverhill when he was killed outright by the bomb. The A.R.P. warden on duty at the time, and the person to find Clifford, was his uncle, Alfred Glazier, who had gone to the Plaza to search for survivors. It became his sad duty to tell his brother Jack that Jack's son had died. He was buried in the civilian war dead area of Hastings Cemetery. Only some time after Clifford Glazier's death did his cousin Brenda Glazier learn this was the reason for her father's initial refusal to her coming home to Hastings after her evacuation to St Albans.[99]

Also killed in this attack was George James Brooker, a blacksmith from Hollington, who was in town on business. He had just been speaking to Fred Heppell, the Plaza Cinema manager who was also killed when the bomb went off, and was killed outright when a piece of shrapnel went through his stomach. His daughter Hilda was sheltering in the underground car park, and she recalls walking through the Memorial in sandals, trying to avoid the vast amount of broken glass from Plummer's windows, frightened of cutting her feet open. She got a bus home and there learned of her father's death. At George Brooker's funeral on 3 October at Church-in-the-Wood, Hollington, the relatives and friends who were gathered at the graveside were shot at by an enemy aircraft. Hilda remembers:

> We were at the graveside saying prayers and I remember several German planes coming over low from the coast and machine-gunning us. We just stood there because there were no trees to hide behind at that time, it was just a graveyard. They shot at us then went back out towards the sea. It was an awful time.[100]

By a tragic coincidence, two brothers were killed within four days of each other in separate air raids on the town. Norman Kemp, a corporal in the R.A.F., had been on leave in town since Sunday 29 to assist in arranging his 33-year-old brother, Nelson Kemp's, funeral.[101] Nelson was killed on 26 September in the air raid on Queen's Road. Sadly, Norman too was killed in Cambridge Road by the Memorial bomb.[102] Norman Kemp had only married in July 1936, when Nelson had acted as best man.[103] The two brothers were buried together in Heroes Corner of Hastings Cemetery on 4 October 1940,[104] although their funeral was not without its own drama. Edwin Barnes and two of his Boys Brigade colleagues, Mr Stevens and Mr Bryant, were walking up Elphinstone Road towards the Mount Pleasant Congregational Church, where the funeral was about to take place, when an enemy aircraft began circling overhead. The three men dived down onto the pavement as an oil bomb was dropped close by, causing no casualties but a big delay to the funeral service.[105]

Narrowly escaping serious injury were Norman Dengate and his uncle, Cecil Dengate, who were on their way from Queen's Road to the Bexhill branch of Dengate's when the bomb struck the Plaza Cinema. They were

31   *Tragic brothers: Nelson and Norman Kemp's graves in Hastings Cemetery.*

32   *Norman Dengate.*

travelling in Cecil's Standard Flying 8 around the memorial when the bomb went off. Norman remembers 'suddenly seeing a big flash up at the top of the building level'. A piece of bomb shrapnel passed through the passenger side of the car in which Norman had been sitting, severing the car door and Norman's overcoat, but miraculously stopping shy of his leg. He did suffer a cut to the back of the neck, which bled profusely, and was taken to a first aid post in Robertson Street opposite Marriott's.[106] Cecil Dengate had glass splinters in his hair from the car's windows and rushed into a hairdresser's to wash it out. On his returning to the street, an air-raid warden grabbed him and took him to a first aid post. His daughter Joan remembers, 'When he was released he was brought up the street and seemed to have aged 20 years.'[107]

A report noted in the A.R.P. logbook on the evening of 30 September again highlights how the continual pounding the town endured was met by people with, perhaps, among the worst jobs of all with resilience and good humour, 'O Peaceful night, could not understand why no warnings, so went down three times to make contact with various policemen who are all convinced that I am mad. P.S. I think I am too.'[108] On a national level, the mood of the country was aptly described thus in the monthly Home Security brief: 'The most marked feature of morale is the toleration, added to humour, with which the impact of war is accepted.'[109]

On 5 October the A.R.P. log records that at 8.20 a.m. there was an 'Incident without warning – Old Town.'[110] Seventeen H.E. bombs, in three separate waves, were dropped on the Old Town, Ecclesbourne Glen, Pebsham and in the sea.[111] In the Old Town, two houses in Old Humphrey Avenue were totally destroyed, four badly damaged but reparable, and eight more in need of evacuation when one of the bombs landed in the cellar of 24 Old Humphrey Avenue.[112] Fortunately for the residents nearby, the bomb had a two-hour time delay so the street was able to be evacuated before detonation at 10 a.m. The house went down into the cellar like a pack of cards, where it remains to this day, the new house having being built directly above it. Living exactly opposite number 24 was the Phillips family. Luckily, Iona Muggridge (née Phillips), her mother and sister were away in Middlesex when the bomb landed, and her father had gone to work:

The front of our house and number five were smashed out, all we got out
of the house was a photograph of me and a photograph of my dad and his
sister. I haven't got anything else, we lost everything. All we had we stood up
in. What didn't get smashed got stolen. They stole furniture and everything.
The back of the house wasn't too bad, but of course you weren't allowed in
here. The Civil Defence and the police were the only ones allowed in. My
dad phoned us and told us we couldn't come back as we had got nowhere
to go. It just hits you, because you don't know if you've got anything left or
not, and of course, when we came home we didn't have anything left. We had
to stay away until my father could get us somewhere to live. What furniture
was left was taken up to what was then Clive Vale School and you had to get
a permit first to go there. I think all there was there was a sideboard and
my mum said, 'Bring down some cups and saucers,' but when I opened the
sideboard, there was nothing there.[113]

Official records describe the property thus: 'Two roofs badly damaged,
contents damaged, long crack near party wall at front. Structure shaken
and shows many cracks in brickwork. Gate piers and fence destroyed. All
ceilings broken.'[114]

Later that morning casualties were suffered when, at 11.29 a.m., a lone
raider dropped 12 bombs which landed in Milward Road, Wellington Road,
Stonefield Road and Wallinger's Walk, and made a direct hit on the *Bedford*

33   *The* Bedford *public house.*

public house in Queen's Road.[115] Lionel Kitchener Goodwin and Annie Payne were killed by falling masonry in the *Bedford*, and Amos Prior was killed by splinters from the blast.[116] In all, eight were killed in this attack and eight seriously injured, several being buried in the pub's wreckage. Number 1 Wellington Road was also totally destroyed by a bomb which killed Richard Reeve Bourn and Florence Elizabeth French.[117]

On 7 October further damage was done when a single H.E. bomb was dropped at 5.56 p.m. on 6 and 7 Stockleigh Road by a lone raider, seriously injuring six people and slightly hurting four others.[118] One man was buried in the rubble until rescue workers finally extricated him at midnight. The *Hastings & St Leonards Observer* had this to say of the rescue:

> The victim was lying cramped in a very confined space, unable to move and bearing already considerable pressure on his body. It seemed only by a miracle that he had not been crushed to death. His foot was jammed in a fall of debris and had sustained some injury ... The man showed magnificent courage and fortitude, joking and laughing from time to time, as the weary hours drew on and he was still not rescued, while the danger of a collapse over his head was as imminent as ever.[119]

On Tuesday 8 October four H.E. bombs and two oil incendiaries were dropped by a lone raider at 4.05 p.m. on the Havelock Road area, killing three people: Mary Frances Monk, Joan Lillian Timms and Arthur Wenman.[120] Twenty-year-old diving champion Mary Frances Monk had been working in an office in Havelock Road when the bomb exploded, ripping the building in which she worked apart. For several days rescuers worked hard to locate her, hoping she might be trapped alive in the building somewhere. When the whole building had been thoroughly checked, and she was not found, her whereabouts became a mystery. Eleven days later, however, her body was finally recovered in the wreck of the adjacent building, having apparently been blown the considerable distance by the bomb blast.[121] Joan Lillian Timms, another of those killed, had been walking opposite Breeds Place with a male companion when a bomb exploded near to them. Her friend flung himself to the ground, escaping with a minor injury, whilst Joan remained standing and was killed instantly.[122] The enemy aircraft then circled over the town attempting to locate the train station. At 4.25 p.m. the aircraft finally dropped a massive 2,000lb bomb, which fortunately landed in the allotments at Braybrooke Road, avoiding major damage or loss of life.[123]

The next few days saw houses destroyed in Canute Road, Fairlight Road, Upper Broomgrove Road, Offa Road, Martineau Lane, Pine Avenue, Stonefield Road, Milward Crescent, George Street, West Hill, Priory Road, Earl Street, Linton Crescent, Edmund Road and Alfred Road.[124] Four people were killed and four were seriously injured in these attacks.[125]

Hastings was ill-equipped to guard against the initial bombings when they came, relying solely upon the work of the R.A.F. to protect the town. Finally, on 14 October 1940, ironically the anniversary of the Battle of Hastings,

35   *Sea Road: A.A. guns ready for enemy action.*

the first A.A. guns arrived in the town to tackle the enemy encroachments. Eileen Parish recalls her reaction to first seeing the guns: 'I can remember getting out of bed and seeing the anti-aircraft guns and I wondered what on earth it was, because you could see it shooting across the sky in the dark.'[126] Soon after the guns' arrival, the raids on the town, and indeed on the country as a whole, started to be predominantly at night.[127]

On Tuesday 22 October, after a high-altitude battle between German and British fighters, one German plane was seen crashing into the sea off Fairlight. The lifeboat was scrambled to search for survivors and picked up the 19-year-old German pilot a few miles from the shore in a rubber dinghy. The Messerschmitt 109 he had been piloting sank minutes after the crash.[128] After the rescue of several German airmen by the Hastings lifeboat, controversy raged over whether the service should be extended to the enemy or not, with several residents arguing in the local paper that it should not. One of the lifeboatmen who rescued a German pilot had been Councillor Wilson, who stressed that the lifeboat service was there to aid any human in danger in the seas, but did also add that he found it difficult to offer the service when the lifeboat had been attacked by enemy aircraft whilst out on service.[129] After one distress call had been received, some of the lifeboat crew said that they would not go out and save the beleaguered Germans, but the coxswain of the lifeboat, John Edward Muggridge, told them that he would take the boat out himself if need be, because he hoped that should the situation be reversed, his life would be saved by a German lifeboat. In the end the whole crew benevolently went out to save the stranded Germans. However, when they reached the shores with the rescued airmen, several old ladies from the Old Town were often waiting on the shore with knives ready to attack the Germans.[130] Les Breach witnessed one such incident: 'I watched an enemy pilot being brought ashore by boat and I particularly noticed he was barefooted and trod on some barbed wire but didn't flinch. Some onlookers booed and hissed at him, but he was guarded by soldiers.'[131]

At 1.45 p.m. on 26 October another lone bomber dropped a salvo of six H.E. bombs and one oil bomb, again on the Halton area, causing widespread destruction, with the Mission Hall and several houses in Priory Road and Albion Street being destroyed. Miraculously, nobody was killed and only four people were injured. Further bombings took place over the following days, with two fatalities and several serious injuries occurring, plus extensive damage to property in the town.[132]

The good fortune of Hastings being nestled between the East and West Hills meant that a great natural resource could be exploited for the protection of a number of Hastings residents in the form of St Clements Caves. In early October 1940, the A.R.P. Committee discussed the plausibility of using the caves as an air-raid shelter for nearby residents, and later, after initial success, as a permanent home for some residents, many of whom had lost their homes in air raids. A meeting on 17 October 1940 of the Committee stated that, 'the Technical Assistant from Regional Headquarters has visited the caves and has authorised the immediate provision of bunks … that he has asked for a scheme to be submitted for new lavatories, heating and the provision of hot water'.[133] A small amount of schooling also took place there. Many of the people using the subterranean shelter were Old Town or West Hill residents, who could easily get there each night or in the event of an air raid.[134] Brenda Glazier and her mother used to walk over the West Hill from St Helen's Road with a neighbouring family, and spend each night in the caves, returning home at seven o'clock in the morning. 'There were bunk beds, two at the bottom, two at the top. My mother and I shared one bunk and our friends slept in the bed beneath us.'[135] An entrance was also opened

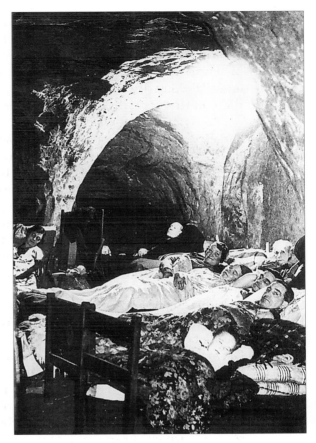

36 *St Clements Caves.*

up in Croft Road for easier access by the Old Towners. Carol Boorman remembers, 'It was very basic but it had a canteen which served tea, coffee and things like that. There were lights in there which I seem to remember were strung along, but it served a purpose.'[136] Carol's brother Les Breach also has recollections of cave life:

> Eventually a school was opened in St Clements Caves for all ages and run by Miss Elvidge. There was a great deal of enemy air activity at that time and we spent many nights in the caves … Living adjacent to St Clements Church, which the siren was placed on, gave us ample warning because the house lights dimmed by 50 per cent as it was activated and we were off to the caves.[137]

For many families the caves were inaccessible, whilst others simply found the subterranean shelter an unsuitable place to dwell, preferring to chance their luck in their own homes. One family who tried the caves but did not like them was the Marsh family of Emmanuel Road. They spent one night there but found them too dank, damp and smelly and so instead preferred to build a blast wall in the kitchen and use three large logs to support the ceiling in case of a collapse.[138]

Despite the attacks on the town, by March 1941 only 200 people per night were staying in the caves, although there was room for 500 or so.[139] With renewed attacks on the town, however, this figure had risen to over 500 people by April 1941, including 126 children over five years old and 57 children under five years old.[140]

After an horrendous five months of change, bombings, overhead battles, and 44 deaths as a direct result of enemy action, and in spite of the almost daily continuation of air-raid warnings,[141] the end of November 1940 bought a temporary lull in the bombings. When the bad weather, which included heavy snow and fierce gales, permitted, the focus of enemy activity became centred on the dreadful Blitz of London. Many Luftwaffe fighter units were also removed to Germany at this time for rest and refit,[142] affording a second relatively quiet wartime Christmas for Hastings.

Three

NIGHT RAIDS, 1941

The New Year was quietly and soberly ushered in without the customary celebrations and partying. Gone were the traditional midnight gathering around the memorial clock tower of crowds bearing witness to the New Year. Despite the deferral of the curfew time from 10.30 p.m. to 1.00 a.m., the town's streets were ghostly quiet, with only the odd reveller on their way home. The White Rock Theatre hosted a dance and several private parties saw in the New Year behind blackout windows, but all in all the mood of the town was one of quiet anticipation that the coming year would bring peace and revert to the happier pre-war days of the 1930s.[1]

Although 1941 would be a year in which the loss of life in Hastings as a result of enemy action would be avoided, the anticipation of peace was sadly without foundation. Enemy raiders began visiting the town more often at night, making their presence more terrifyingly known. Increasingly they were unleashing the incendiary bomb on the town, its purpose twofold: firstly to cause maximum damage and destruction, and secondly to illuminate blacked out areas for subsequent attacks with the more damaging H.E. bombs. Steps were taken nationally and locally to combat the problem. Hastings was split into small sections, over which the A.R.P. wardens had responsibility for the organisation of groups to observe and deal with the incendiary bombs which dropped on the town. Stirrup pumps were issued on a large scale and sandbags were deposited at the base of lamp-posts around the town to smother the fallen devices.[2] Residents were encouraged to form fire-watching parties to protect their own and neighbouring properties. The advice given was that all premises must be easy to enter and that a rake, sand, water and a ladder be to hand so that the fire-bombs could be dealt with quickly. The *Hastings & St Leonards Observer* commented that 'if an incendiary bomb is seen to fall it can be put out by one person in a few seconds, but if it is not seen for 10 or 15 minutes it might require the services of many firemen to extinguish the resulting blaze'.[3] Over 45,000 sandbags were used to protect the town at this time. Sheila Dengate recalls her parents' spirited involvement in preparation for incendiary bombing in their Harold Road home:

My mum and dad were fire wardens and they had to have practices with stirrup-pumps. One night they had a practice in their huge shed in their garden. It was brick-based with glass up one side and there was a fireplace in the end of it, and dad made a very smokey fire in there, and all the neighbours were crawling in on their hands and knees to put this fire out![4]

Soon all business premises in the town had to have a scheme for fire-watching in place, which meant that most businesses in the town needed at least one person to be present throughout the night in case of incendiary attack.[5] Fire-watching, coupled with the necessity to observe the blackout, often made for a frightening and eerie experience. Norman Dengate recalls

37   *Sheila and Gordon Dengate.*

fire-watching once a week at the Dengate's furniture depository in Waterworks Road where, each time bombs were dropped nearby, it was necessary to check the vast warehouse crammed with evacuated families' furniture, armed only with a small torch.[6] Iona Muggridge's father was also a fire-watcher, and she remembers his duties:

> He used to have to spend one night a week fire-watching on Woolworth's roof. If there was a raid at night, my dad and a few neighbours would all rush out the front of the house as the Jerry's were dropping these incendiary bombs, and put them out. Whatever they hit would catch fire, and if you could put the things out you were a lot safer.[7]

Despite air-raid warnings occurring almost daily from 2 January onwards,[8] the first attack of the year came at 8.54 p.m. on 11 January 1941, when 11 incendiary bombs were dropped on White Rock Gardens, the *Medlow Hotel* and Church Road.[9] Fortunately nobody was injured in these attacks. On 12 January, at 8.30 p.m., a lone German raider, a Heinkel 111, encircled the town before randomly machine-gunning along the seafront. The raider was then chased from the town by the R.A.F.[10] Slight damage was caused to a house in the raid but nobody was hurt.[11] The first major attack of 1941 took place at 2.45 p.m. on 31 January when a lone raider dropped three H.E. bombs and two incendiary bombs (two of which failed to explode) in St Leonards, destroying 9 Clyde Road and badly damaging numbers 8 and 10.[12] Only one person was seriously injured in the raid.

For Hastings residents rationing was accepted as a necessity of war, and had to be made the best of, meals being made of anything which could be found. Further additions to the food rationing scheme were made in March 1941, with cheese, marmalade and jams now included.[13] Clothing was also added to the list of rationed items in June 1941. Each man, woman and child received 66 coupons to last a year, with people being encouraged to 'make do and mend' their existing clothing. Later that year tinned fish, meat and vegetables joined the list of rationed goods. Eveline Edwards worked for Sainsbury's at the time and recollects this mandatory aspect of the war:

> I was on the butter counter and it used to come in big blocks which we would pat into little two- or four-ounce rations. We served butter, eggs and custard powder. People used to have to come and get their little bit of butter or marg, then go to the next counter and get their bit of sugar, then they had to go around and get a little bit of bacon, then a bit of cheese. Items like custard powder and one or two things, which were short but which weren't rationed, we used to have a way of marking their ration books for ourselves to know when they'd had these extras, otherwise the same people would get these extras every week. It was a way of life: you just did it. Sainsbury's were a crafty lot; they used to send people around,

38 *Eveline Edwards.*

just like ordinary people doing their shopping, to see if we were doing the right thing all the time. Just to make sure that we weren't giving extra rations. This woman came and she had a serviceman's ration book and she asked for custard powder and I let her have it and I wasn't supposed to. I don't think it was too much of an offence, it would have been worse if I'd let her have extra sugar or something like that.[14]

Some people were lucky enough to have a constant, if slightly mono- tonous, food supply thanks to the nature of the business in which they worked. Eileen Parish's family ran a fish and chip shop in Battle Road, which supplied them with meals each day. Eileen recalls the food situation:

Life was pretty grim with food, the only thing is having a fish and chip shop, we had fish and chips every day – we lived on them for quite a long time. Everything else was very short and my mother wouldn't let me do any cooking because she said we haven't got that much food to spare in case I spoiled it![15]

Joyce Dengate's father was a butcher and slaughterman in Sedlescombe Road North during the war, and so was able to furnish the family with a Sunday roast each week and some variety of meat for mealtimes each day of the week, thereby evading the meagre rations.[16] 'Extras' would sometimes come from the various military personnel stationed around the town, who were not subject to such stringent rationing and would often share what food they had. Derek Hutchinson, who was living in Tower Road West as a boy, remembers the generosity shown by the military: 'Many of the empty, older houses in St Leonards were requisitioned by the army. The house next door to us was an officers' mess for some time and we were able to scrounge food because of the meagre rations we received.'[17] The arrival of the American servicemen later stationed in the town meant that some lucky residents could get food normally unavailable to them. From 26 July 1942 sweets and chocolates were rationed and Cecilie Warren recalls the servicemen giving local children these luxuries: 'They were always pleased to see the local children, we never had to ask for anything. I suppose we reminded them of their own families at home.'[18]

With rationing well established, Hastings turned to other means of food production by turning 'idle acres' around the town into crop-producing war nurseries as part of the nationwide 'Grow More Food' campaign. It was hoped that 100 acres of ploughed land and 15 acres of private gardens would be used to grow such vegetables as potatoes, leeks, carrots, beet, beans, cabbage and onions. The War Agricultural Committee funded the purchase of seeds, equipment and labour, and the corporation were given powers to utilise derelict gardens around the town. Among the areas used for

39 *Joyce Dengate, 1944.*

the production of food were the Harrow Lane football pitch and fields belonging to the Grammar School.[19] The *Hastings & St Leonards Observer* got behind the campaign, showing how small, insignificant areas could yield vast amounts of crops if a little imagination were used. One man's rewarding efforts included using a small piece of derelict land between Havelock Road and Middle Street to grow tomatoes. Arthur Glazier, of 22 Havelock Road, planted 48 tomato plants without using fertiliser, each plant yielding four or five trusses with around 22 tomatoes on each truss. In May 1941, 10 members of the Women's Land Army invaded Hastings and quickly set about turning more unused areas into food production centres. Soon parts of the West Hill and Red Lake recreation ground were dug over and bearing vegetables for the town.[20] Ken Perkins' father was one of many who rented a piece of a field in the Halton area designated for allotments. Ken aided his father in cutting off the surface turf (with turfing irons loaned by the Council) before digging it over for crop plantation.[21]

Although there had been a lull in the bombings since the end of January, members of the public were able to obtain a Morrison shelter free of charge, if their income did not exceed £350 per year.[22] These 6ft 6in. metal cages, which were also known as table shelters, were most often placed in the

40   *The bombed Municipal Hospital, 8 April 1941.*

dining room of the house, to be used upon the sounding of the air-raid
siren. Due to the high number of night raids during 1941, many people
took to sleeping in the shelters each night, regardless of the sounding of
the air-raid sirens. Applications for the shelters were taken in February and
by 24 March 892 had been made.[23] Despite the recent history of bombing
in the town, and the obvious need for such shelters in Hastings, the Senior
Regional Office from the Ministry of Home Security curiously reported to the
A.R.P. Committee that, 'in connection with the distribution of the Morrison
type of indoor shelter in Hastings it is not anticipated that there will be an
early delivery of this type of shelter owing to the need for distribution in the
vulnerable industrial areas'.[24] However, by 2 June 1941 it was decided that
Hastings would be included in the list of vulnerable towns and distribution
would run at 100 shelters per week.[25] Messrs Dengates had the first shelters
on display at their Queen's Road and London Road stores for the public to

view in July of 1941. Joyce Dengate's family had a Morrison shelter in their Clarence Road home which, with the exception of her mother, they all used in the event of an air raid. Her mother refused to climb in and would sit in her chair instead with her tin hat and gasmask on! Some Sundays the local officer of the Salvation Army would come to dinner and if the siren sounded whilst he was there he would dive head-first into the middle of the shelter, leaving no room for anybody else.[26]

After returning home from evacuation, Brenda Glazier recalls her family's Morrison shelter being put to good use:

> I was walking down St Helen's Road with friends and somebody approached me and said, 'Your house has had it,' and, as a child, I was absolutely devastated. When I got home it wasn't as bad as that, the bomb had dropped in the garden so the house was damaged. My mother was at home and there was a neighbour in the house with her and they were in the Morrison shelter. Eventually the house was repaired and we were able to come back. From then on, we carried on as best we could. At night we used to sleep in the Morrison shelter and the neighbours came in as well. I got very nervous and distressed when the sirens used to go at night because my father was fire-watching and I didn't like him leaving us.[27]

Frank Gutsell also experienced the benefits of the Morrison shelter:

> My grandfather had a greengrocery shop in Silchester Road. If we were visiting and there was an air raid, we sheltered in the back room. One such time when we were sheltering, the front door and windows blew in as a bomb had dropped on the house opposite and flattened it.[28]

The night raids continued and Hastings experienced another acute attack, at 2.15 a.m. on 8 April, when an enemy aircraft dropped a staggering 300 incendiary devices, which were themselves highly destructive, around the town. Shortly afterwards another plane followed in behind and dropped 28 H.E. bombs on the town. The fact that there was no loss of life during this raid was nothing short of remarkable, although five people were seriously injured and eight more slightly injured. The attack struck both the Municipal Hospital on Frederick Road and the Royal East Sussex Hospital, as well as Hastings railway station and houses in Priory Road, Stanley Road and Cornwallis Gardens.[29] Providentially, the buildings suffering the worst damage, and classified as 'totally destroyed', included a garage at 36 Priory Avenue, a garden hut at Cornwallis Gardens, and a garden shed at the rear of Upper Broomgrove Road.[30]

Substantially less damage was done to the town thanks to the sterling work performed by the support services and the newly recruited volunteer fire-watchers, for many of whom this was their first taste of tackling incendiary bombs. A Samaritan account of the night's events emphasised just how demanding and problematic their work could be:

41 *The site of the Municipal Hospital, 2004.*

1.45 a.m. – warning. 2.10 a.m. – Loud bang very near. 2.20 a.m. – Eight loud bangs ... 2.35 a.m. M. Tapp and G. Hills return from putting out five incendiaries which fell in woods S.E. of the walled garden at Summerfields. Damage might have proved serious if these had not been dealt with promptly. An improvised extinguisher – a doormat from 'Pooh House' proved very effective ... 2.45 a.m. – Control rang, stated bombs at St Helen's Crescent, Stanley Road and Priory Avenue – some casualties and fires ... 4.20 a.m. – arranged with Mawby to open Citadel [Hastings Salvation Army] at 9 a.m. 4.30 a.m. – All Clear.[31]

A nurse with the Royal East Sussex Hospital, Miss Dorothy Kate Gardener, won the George Medal as a result of her actions when the hospital was bombed. She had been in charge of a private ward and, at the time of the attack, was attempting to usher patients to shelter. When she heard the bombs dropping, she quickly threw herself over a patient, which probably saved the patient's life. Dorothy Gardener suffered severe head injuries during the raid.[32] The *Hastings & St Leonards Observer* published a story about the attacks, an anecdote from which would not have looked out of place in a *Carry On* film: 'The raid was not without its lighter side. The laboratory boy at one hospital rushed up to the Matron after the hospital had been damaged and said: "Oh, Matron, the guinea pigs have escaped!"'[33]

Another hefty barrage of 200 incendiary devices was deposited over the town by a lone German bomber at 3.50 a.m. on 12 June 1941, seriously injuring one man. These bombs again mercifully missed residential areas, landing in Ore Valley, the Mount Pleasant district, and Broomgrove area, narrowly missing the power station there.[34] Mr G.C. Taylor, a fire-watcher, was hit on the shoulder by an incendiary bomb as it pierced the roof of the hut in which he was resting. He suffered severe burns and was taken to hospital in a critical condition. His colleague, Mr F.A. Easter, promptly went to Mr Taylor's assistance, and, although badly burnt on the hands himself, extinguished several other burning incendiaries before being treated.[35]

Some good news was afforded the town at the end of June when permission was given for three sites along Hastings seafront to be modified for sea bathing, allowing locals partial access to the previously inaccessible shores. The three designated areas were opposite Pelham Place, Warrior Square and the west end of the Marina. Constituting only a fraction of the area of coastline previously open to the public, the small area quickly became thronged with people eager to sunbathe on the shore or swim in the sea for the first time in several months, and perhaps to forget, even for a brief moment, the dreadfulness the war had brought the town.[36] Further good news was received when, from Friday 7 November, the ban on visitors to the town was temporarily lifted, so that Hastings residents could have friends and family from outside the town to visit for the duration of the Christmas holiday. It was advised that this concession was retractable at any time, should the political situation necessitate it.[37] It would appear that the government, in lifting the ban on visitors and making concessions on beach access, wanted to portray an outwardly positive view of the threat from enemy invasion at this time, in order to give a much needed boost to morale. But secret Hastings Corporation documents from 1941 and 1942 reveal that plans for the continuation of basic food supplies were drawn up, ready for implementation at any time. In the event of invasion, the town was to be divided into five sectors: Area 1 – Hollington, Bohemia and Silverhill, Area 2 – St Leonards Central and West, Area 3 – Hastings Central, Area 4 – Mount Pleasant, Halton and Ore, and Area 5 – Clive Vale and the Old Town. Shops in each area would be forced to close temporarily whilst stocks were taken, then allowed to re-open under the control of the Emergency Food Officer, who reported to the Town Clerk, D.W. Jackson, from the Town Hall. In the event of the Town Hall being displaced, Winchester House on Gillsman's Hill would be from where local government was controlled.[38] Thankfully this never happened.

On 7 December, the course of the war was to change dramatically when, at 8 a.m., America was devastated by two surprise attacks on Pearl Harbour at the hands of Japanese aircraft, wreaking mass havoc, death and destruction. The attack left 2,403 military personnel and civilians dead, and 1,178 wounded and injured. This single attack was to change the whole direction of the war, pushing it onto a global scale. The following day, America declared war on Japan, closely followed by Britain when Churchill honoured his pact of solidarity. Three days later, Germany and Italy also declared war on America, and gradually country after country joined one side or the other in the conflict.

America joining the war meant that hundreds of U.S. troops were stationed in and around the town in local hotels and houses requisitioned by the military. Undoubtedly their presence would have given a much needed boost to the confidence of the town's remaining residents, and extra income for those beleaguered shops, pubs and restaurants that had managed to remain open.

The rest of the year remained relatively quiet in Hastings, with only one person being seriously injured when an enemy aircraft opened fire on Fairlight Coastguard Station.[39] In view of the fact that this was an isolated incident, it would seem that the aircraft was on a reconnaissance mission or merely passing over and firing randomly at buildings over which it flew. By Christmas of 1941, 38 countries were at war with each other – representing half the population of Earth.[40] In Hastings, over 6,000 houses had been damaged in more than 40 air raids on the town.[41]

Four

TIP-AND-RUN RAIDS, 1942

The year began with a declaration by the Allies which would bind their countries together until total peace and victory had been achieved throughout the world. The agreement of 1 January dictated that none of the nations fighting the Axis would make a separate peace with the enemy, pledging themselves to forming a peace-keeping organisation which would later become the United Nations.

As with the preceding year, the enemy gave Hastings an early taste of what was to come, machine-gunning it out of any complacency which the quiet Christmas might have evoked. On Monday 5 January, two Messerschmitt 109s swept in over the sea and fired arbitrarily at the homes over which they flew. An elderly lady, Miss Nellie Thomas, was leaving her bungalow when the attack happened and several bullets hit her in the leg, which later needed to be amputated. The planes were fired on by A.A. guns and were chased back out to sea by the R.A.F.[1]

With the threat of invasion still high, the local paper published a detailed account of how Hastings' 41,000 residents[2] should deal with enemy parachutists, should the need arise:

> If your enemy holds you up with a revolver and tells you to 'grab for the clouds' and the gun is near you, swing your left arm down, hitting his wrist or gun with the back of your wrist, pushing his arm to his left side, at the same time stepping to your left side. Catch hold of his right wrist (the one with the gun), with your right hand, place your left arm over his right near the shoulder, and break his arm across your chest.[3]

Presumably, had this complex routine been practised sufficiently, it would need to be reversed if the enemy were left-handed and abandoned altogether if there were more than one of them.

The blanket removal of all scrap metal, railings and gates from around the town, to be melted down for munitions, swung into operation in early 1942. All metal found on private property was also to be included, unless its removal would prove to be dangerous. The railings around the Cricket Ground were among the first to go, followed by the remainder of Alexandra

42   *The removal of the railings of St Luke's Presbyterian Church in Silverhill.*

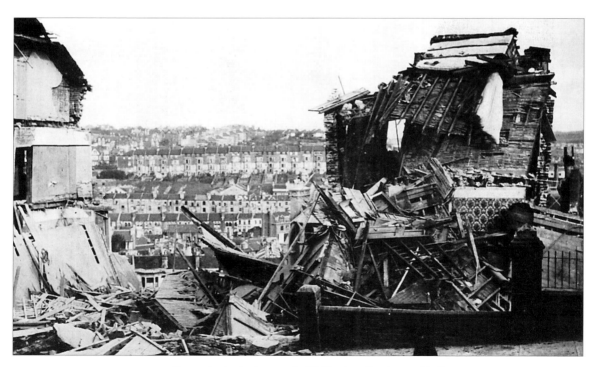

43   *Severe property damage to Wellington Road, 24 April 1942.*

Park's railings (some of which had been taken the previous year), and several churches' railings.[4]

The town's A.A., guns which were lined up along the seafront and at selected points around the town, had remained silent since 5 January but leapt into action once more on 24 April when two Messerschmitt 109s stealthily crept in under low cloud cover, circling the town then descending to less than 100ft and dropping one H.E. bomb each onto the town before heading back out to sea. One bomb fell on the West Hill causing blast damage in George Street and the High Street. The other bomb entirely demolished 11 and 13 Wellington Road, causing three serious casualties.[5] Number

44 *Deirdre Mary Battersby's grave in Hastings Cemetery.*

45 *Emmanuel Vicarage, 3 May 1942.*

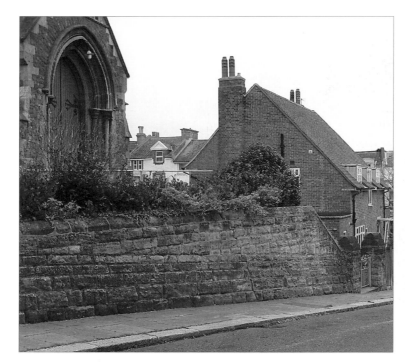

46   *Emmanuel Vicarage, 2004.*

47   *Emmanuel Road after heavy bombing, 3 May 1942.*

48   *Emmanuel Road, 2005.*

9 Wellington Road and 14 Milward Road were so badly damaged by the bomb they were deemed fit only for demolition.[6]

This attack was followed on 3 May 1942 by a bombing raid which left in its wake the first four deaths of the year. Shortly before dark, at 9.05 p.m., four Messerschmitt 109s flew over the town, releasing four H.E. bombs between them, demolishing three houses, and scoring a direct hit on Emmanuel Church and Vicarage. Most windows of the church were blown out, as were several windows of nearby houses.[7] The young daughter of the Reverend Jason Battersby, Deirdre Mary, was tragically killed in the raid whilst she slept in her cot. Mrs Battersby, who, with another daughter, was slightly injured in the attack, stood by until rescue workers had extricated the body of her two-year-old daughter at 1.30 a.m. The sympathy shown to the family by the town was evident at the funeral, when over 200 people were in attendance.[8]

Also killed in the attack were sisters Caroline Harmer Cox, aged 73, and Sarah Ann Cox, aged 78, who died in their home at 24 The Broadway when the building collapsed on them.[9] The sisters had run a general shop there for over 30 years. Eighty-three-year-old James Gamblen and his 78-year-old sister, Mary Gamblen, were buried for several hours in their house at 50 Emmanuel Road, before being pulled dead from the property at midnight.[10] They were buried together in the Borough Cemetery. Twelve people were seriously injured and a further 23 received minor injuries,[11] with numerous properties on The Broadway, Middle Road and Emmanuel Road deemed fit only for demolition.[12]

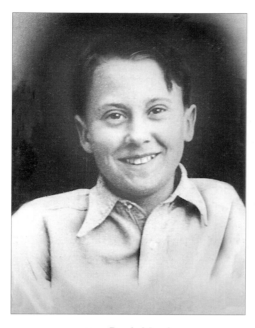

49   *Derek Marsh.*

Derek Marsh was a schoolboy living in Emmanuel Road at the time of the bombing raids who, in competition with a neighbour friend, used to collect bits of shrapnel which landed in the area. He was in his house at the time of the attack and recalls the air-raid siren sounding and then the bombs impacting. After the bombing, he left the house and tried to pick up a piece of shiny shrapnel on his doorstep before his neighbour saw it, but burnt his fingers on it it was so fresh from the explosion.[13]

A divisive change of tactic occurred in March 1942 when fighter-planes were modified to carry bombs. This resulted in what were termed tip-and-run raids whereby, as the name suggests, the German fighter-bomber would tip his bomb load and run back to France.[14] The first tip-and-run raid in Hastings occurred on 17 May, when four Messerschmitt 109s circled the town, machine-gunning the streets in the West Hill area. Twenty-eight-year-old Constance Ethel Torrance was killed when a bullet penetrated the window of her house, 60 St George's Road, leaving a grieving husband and baby daughter.[15] The aircraft then dropped four H.E. bombs: one landed harmlessly in the sea, one in open ground, and two in Havelock Road, which explosion killed 40-year-old Albert Arthur Portsmouth in his home at 42 Havelock Road, which had taken the force of the blast.[16] Eight people were injured in the attacks, two of them seriously, and numbers 40, 41, 43 and 44 Havelock Road had suffered sufficient destruction to warrant demolition.[17]

The relentless tip-and-run raids suffered by the town precipitated many residents' request that Hastings have its own separate air-raid warning system, similar to what had been put into effect in neighbouring seaside towns, such as Bexhill. The current warning system was wholly inefficient for coastal towns, where the enemy could drop its bomb-load and then be over the coast to France before the siren had even sounded. The *Hastings & St Leonards Observer* described the situation rather aptly: 'So far from being heralds they have often been belated banshees wailing out an alert when all the circumstances indicated that "raiders passed".'[18]

On 2 June 1942 a tragic yet, in view of the fast and low flying undertaken by the R.A.F., perhaps inevitable collision of two Spitfires occurred over the town. The accident occurred over the Broomgrove Power Station area and killed the two pilots involved, Sgt Victor Reed and Sgt Robert Guillerman.[19] Guillerman was initially buried in Hawkinge Cemetery, Kent on 5 June, but was exhumed on 14 December 1948 for reburial in France.[20] The accident was put down to a misfortune of war.

The threat from enemy invasion was still high in 1942, and in March a secret meeting took place which formed what was known as 'The Triumvirate' – as the name suggests, a tripartite collaboration of the local authority, the police and the military. The group, comprising the highest town officials, met to discuss the logistics of compulsory evacuation and the necessary retention of key staff in the town.[21] It was decided that 323 key workers should remain in the town, making up rescue parties, decontamination parties, police, first-aid parties, ambulance service and control staff.[22] It was decided that another exercise, dubbed 'The Battle of Hastings', was needed to test communication in the town between the vital services should the enemy land. The mock invasion lasted for 30 hours and involved the military, Home Guard and Civil Defence services. Outsiders may have been rather perplexed at the sight of all entrances to the town being completely blocked, armed soldiers crouching in front gardens with 'snipers' attempting to shoot them. Senior ranks of the local authorities were set problems of major importance, which might have arisen in the event of invasion, sent to them in message form. Among the surviving A.R.P. records from the exercise, which clearly illustrate the situation potentially faced, were:

> Warden reports that enemy dispatch rider passed along Bohemia Road in the direction of Silverhill … Owing to large scale landings of enemy parachutists in all parts of the country they [the military] cannot undertake to send any assistance … must use full initiative to cope with situation and rely on own resources. Reporting a small company of the enemy in a field N. of the Harrow Hill, have informed Home Guard … Poison gas bomb has been dropped at the memorial'.[23]

A message was also received reporting that a fire engine had been captured by the enemy, and was being escorted by enemy tanks through the town.[24]

Once the exercise was over and the lessons learned, the town had a brief early summer reprieve from genuine attack. This ended abruptly when, on 22 August, two Messerschmitt 109s dropped two H.E. bombs on Berlin and Boyne Road, causing 36 casualties, 12 of whom were seriously injured.[25] Eight houses were damaged beyond repair in Boyne Road, Ashburnham Road, and Berlin Road.[26] Joan Fincham witnessed this tip-and-run raid:

> I was out on the East Hill, near my home in Clive Vale, when I heard the raid and I saw the two planes drop their bombs, one of which fell onto my road, Boyne Road. I remember quite clearly, even now, seeing the pile of rubble and debris that rose into the air when the bomb struck the house,

which was about eight doors up the road from my home. I ran home and found smashed windows and other damage had been done, but fortunately my mother and new two-month-old baby brother were safe. We had to leave our house until the damage had been repaired a few days later.[27]

At 4.20 p.m. on Thursday 24 September 1942 came the worst attack seen so far in terms of lives lost. Seven fighter-bombers, with an escort of fighters, swept in low over the rooftops and dropped large bombs at Warrior Square, Quarry Hill, the West Hill and De Cham Road, whilst showering the town with cannon-fire. Twenty-three people were killed and 43 were injured. Among the dead were blind residents Dorothy Dean and Edith Mary Waite in the National Institute for the Blind Home at Quarry Hill, which suffered a direct hit. The residents were being led to an air-raid shelter when a wing of the building bore the full brunt of a bomb, injuring the matron of the home. Many of the dead had been staying at hotels or boarding houses in Warrior Square, which were razed to the ground in seconds, receiving much of the bomb damage. Many people were trapped for several hours under the debris before extrication by the Civil Defence personnel well into the following night. Many houses were also destroyed in West Ascent and West Hill Road in the same strike.

Among the dead were four-year-old Barry Stephen Coltham and five-year-old John Kenneth Tarrant of 7 West Hill, who were killed by the bomb explosion.[28] The following week the *Hastings & St Leonards Observer* ran many of the dead's obituaries alongside several people remembered 'In

50   *Boyne Road after the tip-and-run raid of 22 August 1942.*

51   *West Ascent, 24 September 1942.*

Memoriam' from the town's previous worst attack of 30 September 1940. Despite evacuation and the advances in defence and shelter provision, this attack proved that Hastings was still very much a front-line town, where attacks could take place without warning at any time, leaving in their wake a mass of death and destruction. Yet still the townsfolk continued about their daily lives and dealt with the situation with admirable vigour.

Gordon Dengate remembers going with Dengate furniture removers to one of the houses adjoining those flattened in Warrior Square soon after the incident of 24 September:

> We got called to Warrior Square and a bomb had fallen, and it was amazing how it had happened, it looked as if somebody had just taken a couple of houses out and there was just a gap there. We had to go in the next house up and get the furniture out and the police or Air Raid Warden said to us that the staircase was alright, but whatever we did, not to lean on the wall, what was now the outer wall. It was a bit tricky going up there keeping away from it. I remember that on one of the landings on this outside wall was a big mirror, a massive great mirror, and it was still hanging there and it wasn't broken and yet the whole other side of the wall had gone.[29]

The next tip-and-run attack occurred at 1.23 p.m. on 17 October, when two Focke-Wulf 190s swooped in and dropped two H.E. bombs. St Columbia's Church, which had been used by the A.T.C., was hit, as were a warehouse in Warrior Gardens and several houses in Pevensey Road.[30] In these attacks Alice Sophie Cooper of 43 Pevensey Road died, and Edith Ada Wilmhurst was injured by falling masonry in Pevensey Road and died of her injuries the following day at the Buchanan Hospital.[31] One of the aircraft to carry out the attack was later successfully brought down into the sea by P.O. Gordon Thomas and Sgt Artie Sames of the R.A.F.[32]

In January 1943 Mr Sydney Oak was awarded the George Medal for 'Great courage and devotion to duty' when, as Rescue Party Leader, he went to the aid of a stricken lady trapped under the rubble of her Pevensey Road home on 17 October. Sydney tunnelled into the trapped woman's house and stayed with her for two hours whilst rescue work continued above them, well aware that at any moment the remainder of the house could come crashing down killing both of them. Fortunately, both Sydney and the trapped lady were successfully liberated from the rubble during the night.[33]

Nine days later, a Junkers 88 bomber circled over Hastings for a considerable amount of time, perhaps choosing his target carefully despite coming under heavy fire from the A.A. guns dotted around the town. The aircraft eventually took off out to sea, but rather obstinately returned a few minutes later under cloud cover and released four H.E. bombs on High Beech estate at Hollington, which caused serious injury to one person.[34]

Random machine-gun firing continued on the town and outlying villages toward the end of the year, often only resulting in damage to buildings. Sometimes, however, the enemy would strike civilian targets: on 7 December two women were killed from multiple gunshot wounds in Westfield[35] when a lone raider flew over the village. The first attack was at lightning speed and at a low altitude, with the German raider aiming directly for a block of three isolated houses. The houses were showered with bullets, some penetrating so deeply that they re-emerged the other side. Twenty-eight-year-old Joan Primrose Beeching was in one of the targeted houses of Plumtree Cottages. She was downstairs in the house doing some washing when she was hit by bullets in the head, arms and legs. Her young son, who was asleep upstairs, escaped injury. She was rushed to the Buchanan Hospital but died there the same day, and was later buried in Sedlescombe churchyard.[36] Her next-door neighbour, Mr W. Harthill, narrowly avoided injury, having just left his bed and gone downstairs when the attack took place. Afterwards he inspected his bedroom and found the room and his bed were riddled with bullet holes. Mrs Lewry of Hare Farm Cottage, Brede, was heading for the bus in the same village with her 14-month-old daughter Joyce Elizabeth Lewry in her arms when the attack took place. Upon seeing the enemy aircraft in the vicinity, Mrs Lewry dived into a

52 *Warrior Square after the devastating raid of 24 September 1942.*

nearby shed for shelter but sadly the bullets punctured the shed. Her daughter received several gunshot wounds and was taken to the Buchanan Hospital, but died there the same day.[37] There can be no doubt that this Nazi pilot knew his target was purely civilian, playing no part whatsoever in the war. One wonders how he would have felt knowing that his short burst of fire had just deprived one young boy of his mother, and a young mother of her daughter.

The final death of the year also occurred due to cannon fire, when, at 9 a.m. on 21 December, a German raider fired upon houses at Sedlescombe Road North, Marline Avenue, Madeira Drive, St Helen's Road, Bexhill Road and Bulverhythe Road. Beatrice Harriett Walker was killed at 140 Sedlescombe Road North by a gunshot wound.[38]

Hastings' fourth wartime Christmas offered a flicker of reminiscence of pre-war times, and a hint of perhaps what future Christmases might bring the town, as church bells peeled merrily on Christmas morning, as had been forbidden for so long.[39] The Christmas holiday, however, was definitely the calm before the storm of 1943.

Five

THE WORST ATTACKS, 1943

As if it were needed, the outlying villages to Hastings received warning that they were not beyond the reaches of the enemy when they were the first to suffer enemy action in 1943 in the shape of two (later crashed) aircraft on 4 January. At 12.54 p.m., three Focke-Wulf 190s dropped bombs at Winchelsea. One of the aircraft began machine-gunning three land-girls who were busy working in the fields in Winchelsea. The land-girls, Pamela Hayward, Doreen Wilson and Betty Pullmore, sought refuge in a nearby shed, and the only casualties were a pony, which was killed, some cattle, which sustained injury, and the pilot of the aircraft.[1] He had been flying so low that he hit overhead telephone cables, sending the plane crashing to the ground at Castle Farm, Winchelsea.[2] The pilot, 25-year-old Fw. Herbert Müller, died at the scene, and was buried on 8 January, with four other German aircrew who died the same day, in Hawkinge Cemetery, Kent.[3]

Later that day a German Dornier 217 came over the Channel at low level and crashed into high ground at Furze Hill.[4] The damaged aircraft, which had been laying mines in the Channel along with 13 other enemy aircraft,[5] apparently lost its bearings, then continued before crashing into an empty bungalow, Heath Cottage, tearing the building in two. The four crew, Hartmut Eucker, Ernst Kern, Kurt Tomczyk and Rolf Fischer, died instantly in the accident. They were taken to Hawkinge for burial.[6] The horrific scene of wrecked aircraft and airmen is captured in the photograph on page 72. After the accident, local residents sat for photographs on a fuel tank from the stricken aircraft before they realised that it was in fact an unexploded parachute mine.

Guestling was the next village to receive an attack, at 9.10 a.m. on 9 January, when four Focke-Wulf 190s executed a swift tip-and-run raid. With guns blazing, they released three H.E. bombs over Guestling. One landed directly on a bungalow near to the *White Hart Inn*, killing its three occupants, 80-year-old Mrs Margaret A. Elliott, her daughter, Miss W.M. Elliott, and their maid, Miss M. Bashford. Mrs Elliott was the widow of Reverend Ernest

53   *Macabre scene at Fairlight after the Dornier crash of 4 January 1943.*

54   *Graves of Hartmut Eucker, Ernst Kern, Kurt Tomczyk and Rolf Fischer, Hawkinge, Kent, 2004.*

W. Elliott, vicar of Fairlight church from 1903 to 1925, and the daughter of Reverend Henry Stent, vicar of Fairlight from 1857 to 1903.[7]

Hastings' first direct hits came at 8.00 p.m. on Sunday 17 January, when two H.E. bombs were dropped on Fairlight Place and Tilekiln Cottage, fortunately causing no casualties.[8] The subsequent attack came on Thursday 28 January when two enemy fighter-bombers made a tip-and-run raid on the town.[9] A husband and wife had a remarkable escape from serious injury when one of the bombs ricocheted off a chimneystack, flew 100 yards through the couple's De La Warr Road house, passing through the French windows at the rear of the property and their garden fence, before coming to rest and exploding on a golf course behind the house. The bomb passed by both the wife, who was in the kitchen writing a letter to her soldier son, and her husband, who was tending to his garden.[10]

On the morning of 9 February four H.E. bombs were dropped (two failed to explode) by two bombers taking advantage of bad weather and cloud cover. One bomb demolished the main section of St John's Church in St Leonards, leaving only the tower and spire standing.[11] Houses were also affected in Alfred Road, Ashbrook Road and Moscow Road, which took a direct hit. Fifty-six-year-old Ethel Alice Fowler of seven Moscow Road was injured at home from gunshot wounds, and died the following day at the Municipal Hospital from her injuries. Also at 7 Moscow Road were 64-year-old Sarah Martin and her four-year-old granddaughter, Ann Rosemary Watson, who were killed by flying debris from the bomb blast.[12] They were buried together in Hastings Cemetery on 13 February.[13]

Death and destruction came to Hastings on 11 March 1943, in the heaviest and worst raid it would see throughout the war. Between 3.32 p.m. and 3.36 p.m., 20 Focke-Wulf 190s crossed the Channel at Fairlight then came in line abreast at 'zero feet' (rooftop height), while a further eight Focke-Wulf 190s patrolled just off shore. This spectacular scene must have frightened residents immensely, as a salvo of 25 powerful H.E. bombs were dropped randomly over the town. Beachy Head and Dungeness R.A.F. patrols were immediately scrambled to counter this attack, as were all available units from Squadrons 609, 308, 64, 403 and 91. The latter three sighted 12 of the enemy aircraft after the attack and gave chase as far as the Somme, but did not succeed in engaging fire. Two Focke-Wulfs, according to official documents, were destroyed by A.A.

55　*The lucky husband and wife outside their wrecked De La Warr Road home.*

guns. Allied pilots engaged in the attack later stated that the enemy aircraft were effectively camouflaged with a light-grey glossy paint, making them difficult to see at sea level.[14]

One pilot who flew several tip-and-run raids against England was Lt Leopold Wenger, who took many pictures from his plane, including the amazing photograph opposite of Hastings moments before he dropped his bomb load, which, as Chris Goss suggests in *Luftwaffe Fighter-Bombers over Britain*, was 'an amazing feat for a lone pilot, flying at low level and high speed and running the gauntlet of the British ground and air defences'.[15]

The devastation inflicted upon the town was unprecedented, with 38 people losing their lives, 39 seriously injured and 51 slightly injured.[16] Silverhill suffered particularly badly as many buildings were completely wrecked, including the (mercifully empty) St Matthew's School, which took a direct hit. Houses were destroyed in Battle Road, Bury Road, Perth Road, Sedlescombe Road North, Strood Road, Combermere Road, Springfield Road, Aldborough Road, Clarence Road, Salisbury Road, Bohemia Road, Holmesdale Gardens, King Edward Avenue, Broomfield Road, Queen's Road, Wallinger's Walk, Alma Villas and Alma Terrace.[17] Eileen Parish recalls witnessing the severe Silverhill bombings:

My friend Mrs Levett in Perth Road was bombed. She was sitting by the
fire when it happened and was burnt all down one side. She later told me
that when the firemen were hosing the house, she was trying to catch the
water in her mouth because she was so terribly thirsty. She was trapped in
the house and it took them a long time to dig her out. She was very badly
burned, but she was a tough old bird. Her daughter lived down at London
Road and I wanted to tell her what had happened. It was my 21st birthday
that day. My uncle, Charlie Bristow, drove past and picked me up, he told
me he spent his 21st birthday on the firing line in the previous war. We
had to go miles, all through Ore just to get to London Road because of
the bombings.[18]

Eileen later went past the Hollington Police Station on Battle Road and
saw bundles of bedding hanging from a broken window. Apparently what
had occurred was another of the strange incidents caused by the low-flying
aircraft, which jettisoned their bombs at such an acute angle. The bomb had
passed through the front of the Police Station, scooped some linen from
the empty bed in the room, then passed through the window, continuing
its journey until it finally detonated in Adelaide Road.[19] Eileen later spoke

56 *Seconds prior to devastation: Hastings photographed from the cockpit of Wenger's
aircraft, 11 March 1943, day of the worst attack. Marine Court can be seen to the right
of the picture.*

57   *A policeman surveys the scene at Adelaide Road after the 11 March 1943 attack.*

to somebody who was dangerously close to the explosion: 'He said he can remember being blown over the houses and that he was looking down at the houses, but he got away from it without much injury.'[20]

Schoolgirl Brenda Glazier also remembers seeing the devastation caused by the attacks and the subsequent effect on one of her friends:

> I walked home through Silverhill and it had been virtually destroyed on this Thursday afternoon. The headmistress got us together in groups to walk home and I can remember somebody coming walking up the road and seeing this girl who was with me, and saying to her, 'Don't you come down now dear, not now, you go back to school.' Her father was killed that afternoon.[21]

The Morrison shelters proved many times their worth throughout the town, and there are numerous stories of lives being saved because of them. John Bristow's uncle's house in King Edward Avenue was among those hit on 11 March 1943. His two aunts, who were busy preparing the house for their other sister's arrival with her newborn baby, had their lives saved by a Morrison shelter. John recalls the day:

My aunts, Mrs Gear and Mrs Gibbs, got into the Morrison shelter as soon as the air-raid siren sounded. One dog always ran in the shelter when the sirens sounded, but the other dog wouldn't come in and he was killed when the house was hit. They were buried in the shelter, but were later dug out.[22]

For Brenda Wallis, the 11 March attack came dangerously close to her and her family in Sedlescombe Road North:

The air-raid siren went but the bombs started dropping almost as soon as the siren had gone, we didn't get very much of a warning. I was actually with my grandmother and she'd got one of these Morrison shelters and we'd got my aunt's five-month-old baby with us. I remember when all this crashing started and I pushed grandma into the Morrison shelter and I put the baby in with her then scrambled in with them until it had all died down. When I got out, all the dust and dirt was coming down from the sky all around, bits of feather mattresses and beds were coming down and settling everywhere.[23]

Among those killed was Mrs Emma Riggs Hoad, a teacher in the town for over 30 years,[24] who was killed at her home at 41 Adelaide Road by the bomb blast.[25] Another retired teacher, Miss Emma Louisa Giles, who had been headmistress of Silverhill School, died at her home at 52 Vale Road.[26] Many other sad and tragic losses were sustained in this attack, including several children.

Although the suffering and ruin had been great, neighbours aided their distraught or homeless friends and the voluntary organisations provided meals and a place to stay for those who needed it. It is fair to say that the people of the town showed great defiance in the face of the enemy during such incomprehensible destruction and chaos. Spirits were raised the following week by a surprise visit by the Duchess of Kent, who, after a private lunch at Summerfields with corporation dignitaries, inspected various branches of the Civil Defence, chatted with bombed-out victims in the Filsham Road rest centre and visited those sheltering at St Clements Caves. She offered her sympathies to affected townsfolk, and had the reciprocal sympathy of those with whom she spoke, for she herself was in mourning for her husband, the Duke of Kent. Word quickly spread of her low-key arrival and crowds gathered to catch a glimpse of Her Royal Highness about the town.[27]

The Easter holidays were the first since the declaration of war which did not languish under the coastal defence ban that had been imposed for the three previous years. Ironically, although visitors were allowed to visit the town, most stayed away and local businesses, boarding houses and hotels reported the quietest Easter break on record.[28] Perhaps people stayed away from Hastings after the horrendous attack of 11 March, fearing further such large-scale attacks in the future?

In mid-April the newly appointed coxswain of the Hastings lifeboat, John Edward Muggridge, was killed in Rye Harbour when he accidentally

58   *Damage to the Old Town.*

trawled up a mine. He had recently been invalided out of the Navy and bought a fishing boat, which he had not had long before his untimely death. Unfortunately, neither he nor fellow lifeboat crew member William Hilder got to collect their bronze medals for the rescue of two people stranded at sea on 7 December 1940.[29] His daughter-in-law, Iona Muggridge, remembers his tragic death:

> There were three of them on his boat and this mine blew them to pieces, and all they found was a foot and a sea boot. His father was Chief Coastguard at the time and he said, 'Whoever has bought that ashore, get back in that boat and take it back to where the rest of them are and I dare any of you to bring any bits back ashore. Leave them alone, the three of them, leave them be.' There were some people who wanted the bits to be buried, but like my husband's grandfather said, you can't bury a foot because you don't know who it belongs to.[30]

Two months after the 11 March attacks, disaster was to strike once more with the second worst raid on the town. At 12.59 p.m. on Sunday 23 May, 10 Focke-Wulf 190s swept in at rooftop height, machine-gunning the town at the same time as releasing 25 bombs,[31] which scored direct hits

59   *Damage to the Old Town.*

60   *Damage to the Old Town.*

61   *The destruction at the* Swan Hotel, *23 May 1943.*

on five public houses and two hotels filled with diners. Twenty-five people were killed in this Hastings raid, 30 were seriously injured and 55 slightly injured.[32] The High Street in the Old Town suffered particularly badly, with many of the deaths occurring at the *Swan Hotel*, which was packed with lunchtime customers. Rescuers worked tirelessly throughout the night and following day, recovering only one person and a dog alive from the rubble. One of the dead was William Hilder, a mechanic and engineer for the Hastings lifeboat who had been part of the crew to take the Hastings lifeboat to Dover in preparation for the Dunkirk evacuation. He was killed by falling masonry as the building collapsed around him.[33] The bodies of the licensee John Gummerson's wife, Grace Rosina Gummerson, sister, Hilda Gummerson, and three-year-old son, Trevor Ernest Gummerson, were recovered the following day. The *Warrior Gate* public house also suffered badly when, after taking a direct hit, the building burst into flames. A number of people were trapped in the buildings, and some were killed, including Albert Henry Reader, the manager of Plummer Roddis.[34] The fire

62 *The site of the* Swan Hotel, *2004, which has been left as a garden in memory of those who lost their lives there; and the memorial plaque which can also be found on the site.*

brigade were quickly on the scene to put out the fire and rescued the licensee, his wife and a customer from the wreckage of the basement. *The Queen's Hotel* was graced when a bomb struck the top storey, before crashing into the *Albany Hotel* next door. Over 100 people who filled the bars and restaurant had their lives spared, with only five minor injuries from glass splinters.[35] Houses were completely destroyed, or only fit for destruction, after the raid in Swan Terrace, the High Street, Castle Street, Pelham Street, White Rock, Norman Road, London Road, Saxon

63   *John Bristow.*

64   Denmark Arms *in Denmark Place, one of five public houses to be hit on 23 May 1943.*

65 The Albany
Hotel, *23 May 1943*.

Street, Grand Parade, Gensing Road, Undercliff and St Clements Place. Two of the enemy aircraft which carried out the attack were brought down: one, piloted by Ofw. Herbert Dobroch, was hit by a Typhoon from No. 1 Squadron, and the other, piloted by Fw. Adam Fischer, was hit by flak. A simultaneous attack by 10 Focke-Wulf 190s was carried out on Bournemouth, stretching an overwhelmed R.A.F.[36]

For John Bristow, who was in town with a friend when the attack occurred, the events still remain crystal clear in his mind:

I don't remember how many aircraft there were, but they were strung out
wing-tip to wing-tip along the coast. I was walking down by the Post Office
when the guns opened up. There was a 40mm Bofor gun on the old *Hastings
Observer* office, and he opened up just as we were walking past. There was a
god-almighty explosion and we went into the passage by *The Havelock* pub,
and we dived into that passage and threw ourselves onto the ground and
lay there looking out before a bomb hit what was the old *Royal Oak Hotel*.
Along by Woolworth's there was a car going by and it was sent up into the
air by the bomb and over and over. I learnt later that it was Mr Johnson
in there, a chap I knew very well; he was killed. While we laid there, there
was another terrific explosion down the side of Plummer's and I'll never
forget seeing a huge lump of yellow-coloured masonry come over and land
on the tram wires. It landed on these tram wires and it went down to the
ground then straight back up again. I saw the wires stretch down and then
up and back it went. I never knew where it went to, but it was a huge lump
of masonry! When it had quietened down we went through to Robertson
Street onto the grounds of the *Albany Hotel* and this Canadian soldier came
running over covered in blood and dirt. He picked up his motorbike which
was lying on its side in the gutter, and dashed off towards Bexhill, about
80 miles an hour.[37]

Minor attacks on the town continued throughout the year, but after
a very successful attack, from the enemy's point of view, on Eastbourne
on 6 June 1943, the highly orchestrated tip-and-run attacks inexplicably

66   *Reeves Corner, 23 May 1943.*

67 Queen's Hotel *after the 23 May 1943 attack.*

68 *The* Plough Inn, *Crowhurst, after the bomb of 16 October 1943.*

69 *The* Plough Inn, *Crowhurst, 2004.*

ceased.[38] Enemy aircraft were continually flying over the town, sometimes on reconnaissance missions and sometimes merely passing over en route to London,[39] which is often when bombs would be dropped arbitrarily on the town. Compared to the previous two, what was a relatively minor attack took place when 14 H.E. bombs were dropped at 5.20 p.m. on 9 July by a lone raider in the areas of the Grange, Harley Shute, Charles Road, Cumberland Gardens, Brittany Road, Markwick Terrace, Dane Road and The Green. There was only one slight injury from the attack.[40] The official report from No. 11 Group Fighter Command, which defended the south east, described the raid thus:

> Of about 10 e/a [enemy aircraft] operating, 7 believed Dornier 217s, crossed the coast during the afternoon between Beachy Head and Dungeness at heights ranging from 1,000-3,000 ft, and operated over Kent, Sussex and Surrey. Bombs were dropped at East Grinstead where a direct hit was scored on a cinema, and other H.E.s were dropped at Hastings, Orpington, Croydon and near Biggin Hill aerodrome. Weather was 6-60/10ths cloud from 700 to 1800 ft in the area, and 10 s/e [single-engine] and 6 t/e [twin-engine] fighters were put up. Two Do.217s were destroyed through joint efforts of the R.A.F. and A.A. and a Mosquito of 85 Sqdn also crashed, the crew being killed.[41]

After three years of bombardment by and attacks from enemy aircraft, Hastings finally got the advanced warning system for which it had fought in August 1943. The 'cuckoo' warning system operated independently of the national air-raid siren with its own 'all clear' signal.[42] It was, however, too late: the worst attacks on the town were over. However, the system arrived at a time when the number of people in the town was on the increase once again following the realisation that invasion was now very unlikely. Residents had been slowly filtering back since the population plummeted in September 1940. By August 1943 the population stood at around 37,000, just over half of the pre-evacuation figure. There were 1,207 licensed food shops open in August 1940, a figure which was down to just 662 by August 1943. The number of boarding houses for the same periods was 318 and 60 respectively, with the largest ones remaining closed.[43] Indeed many small businesses were forced into closure. Those who were fortunate enough to stock non-rationed items often did a roaring trade. Eileen Parish recalls the unpredictability of customer volume at Greenwood's fish and chip shop in Battle Road:

> People started dribbling back [to the town] and I remember the first night we opened the shop we took five shillings. Then of course when there were people here, we used to get queues. The people used to queue a long way from the shop, waiting for fish and chips because it was food. We got all our food away, it used to come from Grimsby: if we ordered it, we got it, which was quite surprising.[44]

Finally some good news regarding the political situation arrived in the town and throughout the country via the BBC 6 o'clock news on Wednesday 8 September. It was announced that Italy had surrendered unconditionally to the Allied forces, inflicting substantial damage to the once-powerful Axis. The *Hastings & St Leonards Observer* commented that the town greeted the news 'without demonstration, but in a mood of cheerful and sober satisfaction, the BBC announcement of the good tidings ... brought a thrill to every local home'.[45]

Despite the weakening of the Axis with the capitulation of Italy, the attacks on the country were far from over. Crowhurst came under attack on 16 October 1943, when an enemy aircraft, believed to be a lone Focke-Wulf 190, dropped an H.E. bomb on the village from 900 feet,[46] leaving a nine-foot crater on a green in front of the *Plough Inn* which, fortunately, was not as crowded as it would have been later that evening.

The bomb caused three fatal casualties: 40-year-old Frank Wigglesworth and an elderly couple, Arthur and Adelaide Parks, all died as a result of the bomb blast. Arthur Parks, it was believed, was standing at his garden gate when the bomb fell close to his home, which suffered severe damage. The landlord of the *Plough* and his wife were seriously injured in the attack, because the roof of the pub was damaged and all the windows blown in.[47] June Kemp was witness to the attack and remembers, 'That bomb dropped at 9 o'clock at night. I was on my way, cycling along the road, to pick up my sister-in-law, who had been to Hastings and didn't like coming along the road on her own. I dived in the hedge to get out of the way – so frightening.'[48]

Four more attacks were made on Hastings during the final two months of 1943; all of them were at night and only damaged property. The final raid of the year occurred on New Year's Eve when the recreation hut on Bulverhythe Recreation Ground was demolished by a bomb.[49]

Six

THE FINAL RAIDS,
D-DAY AND THE DOODLEBUG ERA, 1944

Raids in 1944 began at 2.30 a.m. on 5 January, when a single H.E. bomb was dropped on Filsham Road,[1] near Braeside, the house of 72-year-old Hastings surgeon, Mr Ligat, who had just returned from a midnight emergency operation at the Royal East Sussex Hospital. Having garaged his car, he was about to enter the house when the bomb exploded on open ground next to his house, the blast blowing off his right arm. His wife escaped injury, but his daughter was injured in the blast and considerable damage was done to his house.

After this raid there was a welcome lull in the attacks on the town – until 1.28 a.m. on 12 March, when a single H.E. bomb was dropped on numbers 22 and 24 Priory Road opposite Emmanuel Church,[2] seriously injuring three people and killing five: Edward Leslie Badham, his daughter Dorothy May Badham, five-year-old Bryon John Saunders and his parents, Ethel Mary and George Saunders.[3]

Mr Badham, who died in hospital soon after being extricated from the ruins of his house, was a well-known and respected artist and art teacher in the town and had, among his many achievements, been elected in February 1941 an Associate of the Royal Cambrian Academy, the Welsh National Academy of Art.[4] Emmanuel Church was once again damaged by the blast of the bomb, and several houses suffered roof and window damage in Alpine Road, Collier Road, Croft Road, Emmanuel Road, Plynlimmon Road, Priory Road and Vicarage Road.[5] The raids were not without their lighter sides though: the *Hastings & St Leonards Observer* reported that an elderly lady returned to her terraced home, which had been damaged during this raid, to check on her parrot. When she uncovered the bird he exclaimed, 'Look at the kitchen, look at the kitchen'.[6] At an A.R.P. meeting, Councillor Raby stated that he had been asked by Westhill residents to express their appreciation at the way in which the Civil Defence services carried out their duties on 12 March. It was also mentioned that the police would be asked why children had been allowed to roam freely over the bomb site after this incident.[7]

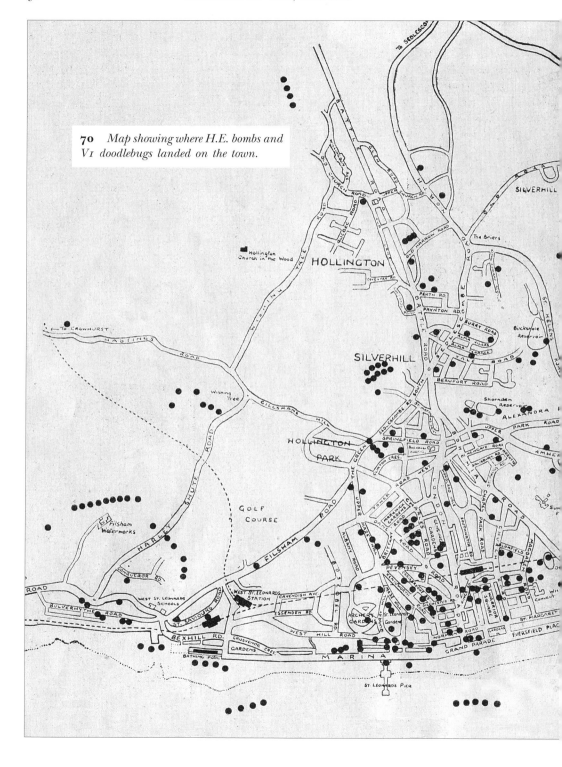

70 *Map showing where H.E. bombs and V1 doodlebugs landed on the town.*

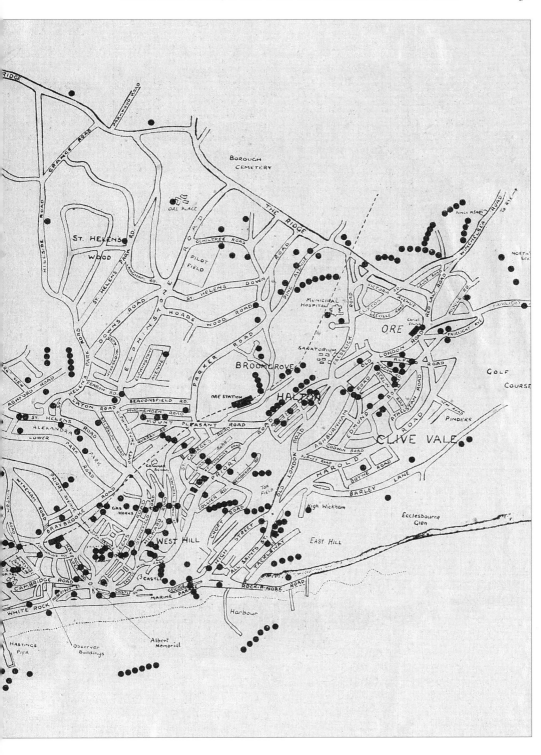

Three years and eight months after the first bombing raid on Hastings, a significant milestone was reached, although it was not known at the time, when the final H.E. bomb landed in the town at 11.50 p.m. on Monday 27 March 1944. The bomb seriously injured one person when it exploded in Filsham Road.[8] Although this was the final H.E. bomb dropped, the town did not entirely escape attack after the flying bomb (or doodlebug as it became known) made a brief but deadly appearance in a final, futile attempt by the Nazis to win the war.

On Saturday 22 January a German bomber, a Heinkel 177, was brought down in the sea by an 85 Squadron Mosquito nightfighter, the 23-year-old airman parachuting clear of the plane and landing in a vicarage garden in Hastings.[9] Fireman Mr R. Wise had this to say of the incident:

> I was on my way to report at my station after having heard bombs fall, when I saw a plane come down in flames over the sea. It skimmed along just above the water and dived into the sea, and immediately there was a tremendous explosion. As I was going along the road a woman, who was on fire-guard duty with her daughter, called my attention to something white hanging on a telephone pole and making a flapping noise. It was, of course, pitch dark and I thought it was a parachute flare that had caught in the wires. I went past without seeing the airman who was apparently against a wall inside the garden between the pole and a tree. As I went to him he stood up and put his hands down to his pockets and for a moment I thought he was feeling for his pistol. But he came forward and raised his hands and when I put my hands over his tunic he said, 'No gun.'

Mr Wise informed the police who took the airman into custody.[10] Of the crew of six, only two survived the crash: Fw. Beitter and Ofw. Andrae.[11]

On Saturday 1 April, under orders from the War Secretary, Hastings, along with other coastal areas, once again became a prohibited area to visitors.[12] The ban, extending from Land's End through to The Wash in Norfolk, was not this time implemented from fear of invasion, but rather as a precaution in preparation for D-Day (although this reason was obviously not expressed to the public at the time). The ban effectively killed off any hopes for Easter trade in the town and promised a bleak outlook for the coming summer season. Spirits were raised, however, when the Prime Minister, Winston Churchill, along with Mackenzie King and General Smuts, visited Hastings on the evening of Friday 12 May. For obvious reasons, the event was not reported in the local newspaper until 24 June. Crowds of people swarmed the town's streets, lining the route and waving Union Flags, eager to catch a glimpse of the man who had given inspiration and hope that the country could survive this atrocious time to so many. Churchill himself was in very high spirits according to the local paper,[13] perhaps thanks to the continuing successes racked up by the Allied troops so far, or perhaps to the impending D-Day landings, which would start to seal an Allied victory.

Finally, four years to the day after Churchill made his 'We shall fight them' speech, the long-anticipated 'Second Front' came on the night of 5 and morning of 6 June 1944, as Allied troops headed to the south coast in preparation for Operation Overlord. In a satisfyingly marked change, the skies over Hastings were crowded not with the usual hostile enemy aircraft, but with Allied aircraft on their way to aid the impending invasion.[14] More than 4,000 Allied boats and landing craft filled the Channel on their way to Normandy. June Kemp recalls the dozens of lorries and war vehicles, full of personnel, driving stealthily through Crowhurst village on the night of 5 June, on their way via the back roads to the D-Day landings: 'It was full of English soldiers and they were coming from somewhere right out. This convoy came through and it was all night long. Nobody knew where they were going, it was all hushed and you daren't say anything.'[15] The 'say nothing' sentiment was echoed by Hastings resident Iona Muggridge, who was a telephone operator for the R.A.F., stationed at the time in Brighton:

> It's amazing what you get to hear, you're not told properly, but you hear this and you hear that, and draw your own conclusions. We knew something was going on because about a fortnight before D-Day, we were moved up to Padgate in Lancashire as they cleared the entire coast. I'd signed the Official Secrets Act, so I couldn't say anything about it.[16]

Gordon Dengate witnessed the Channel 'chock-a-block' with boats on their way to the D-Day landings,[17] a pleasing sight also witnessed by Joan Fincham, who remembers going up onto the East Hill with friends and family to watch the ships gather. 'Then we knew that victory and peace were not so very far away.'[18]

Despite sustaining heavy losses, the Allies successfully broke through northern France, which signalled the beginning of the end. After the successful landings, Hitler wanted to exact a last-ditch revenge on Britain. According to Matanle, 'From 1942 onwards, Hitler frequently told those who dared to express doubt in the eventual German victory that the war would be decided by Germany's secret weapons, against which there would be no defence.'[19] His secret weapon came in the form of the V1s (*Vergeltungswaffe Eins* – Revenge Weapon 1). Although they did cause acute damage, destruction and loss of life throughout the country, Hitler had vastly underestimated the skill and dexterity of the R.A.F. and A.A. batteries in the south east, which meant the damage was severely reduced. The allies quickly gained the upper hand in the battle against the V1s, using ingenious techniques to destroy them.

Instructions given to the police, wardens and the R.O.C. read,

> The pilotless aircraft is believed to resemble a small monoplane having a wing span of about 20 feet and an overall length of about 18 feet. No pilot's cockpit will be visible. The aircraft will be jet-propelled and consequently no propeller will be fitted. Maximum speed: Is likely to exceed 400 mph.[20]

The first doodlebug to appear in the skies over England came at 4.08 a.m. on 13 June 1944.[21] Initially the Folkestone R.O.C. post spotted something in the sky heading over the Channel, which they incorrectly identified as an aircraft on fire. It was spotted at Martello Tower 24, the R.O.C. post in Dymchurch, by Archie M. Wraight and Ernest E. Woodland. Bob Gearing's father, Arthur James Gearing, was the head of the R.O.C. post and he too witnessed the first doodlebug through binoculars from his bedroom window in Dymchurch. Bob Gearing recollects:

> My uncle Archie Wraight saw it, and had been told that there was something, a secret weapon, expected, and when he saw it, he immediately said, 'Diver, diver, diver' over the air which was the code word for the secret weapon. Before it was five miles out from Dymchurch he had reported it and that went through to Maidstone, then to Uxbridge. They were congratulated as they reported it before it reached the coast.[22]

The first V1 to hit Britain eventually landed in Swanscombe, Kent.[23]

The first to land locally was at 12.47 a.m. on 16 June 1944, when it came down at Glyne Gap causing minor damage but no casualties.[24] The air-raid alert was sounded and lasted for over 12 hours, until noon that day.[25]

Although the doodlebugs were a deathly menace, people quickly became blasé about them, all the while listening out for the thunderous sound of the engine hurtling above them, which Bob Gearing likened to the sound of a very loud motorbike engine.[26] Hastings residents' experiences of the flying bomb vary greatly but, for the most part, they combined safe observation with an apprehension of the notorious sound of the engine cutting out and

71 *Archie Wraight (right) and Arthur James Gearing on duty at the R.O.C. Post, Dymchurch.*

72 *Joyce Wedge with her father.*

the rocket careering towards the ground. Such a time is recollected by Joyce Wedge, who was cutting through a wooded path in Alexandra Park on her way to her Junior School in Silverhill when a doodlebug came over:

> Its engine cut out and we had all been told if we were out in the open and this happened to get onto the ground, but a lady was shaking out a rug in her front garden and called us to run in, and we stayed with her for the explosion and then went off to school![27]

On the occasions when a doodlebug succeeded in getting to the coast past the A.A. guns, then Allied aircraft would often either shoot down the robot, or, using a tactic which required great skill, fly alongside it and, once safely over open countryside, tip the aircraft's wing beneath that of the doodlebug's wing, thus sending it to an early and safe demise

and preventing it wreaking havoc
in London or other built-up areas.
This spectacle was witnessed by
many locals on several occasions,[28]
although, fatal mistakes could sometimes occur with this technique, as
will be seen later in this chapter.
After the first few days, the R.A.F.
were taking down around 50 per
cent of the flying-bombs, but within
a fortnight the figure had increased
to an exceptional 80 per cent. Wing
Commander Roland Belmont, leader
of three Tempest wings to target the
flying bombs, claimed over 600 'kills'
divided almost equally between each
wing. By mid-July, five A.A. batteries
had been established in the town,
helping the R.A.F. to shoot down the
flying bombs.[29]

73   *Brian Bristow.*

At the start of the flying-bomb era,
Gordon Dengate wanted to chance
his luck and go with his father, Leslie,
on a furniture removal job to London
to see the doodlebugs:

> You used to do these things and didn't worry about it. I remember helping
> to carry a wardrobe down the staircase and I was at the top holding it and
> another fellow at the bottom, and a doodlebug came over and the engine
> cut out. The next thing you knew there was a terrific bang nearby, and I
> was standing there holding this wardrobe and I couldn't do anything about
> it! The thing came down nearby, but not too near to us.[30]

Annette and Cathleen Munn's mother had a novel approach to defence
against the doodlebugs:

> Our mother would walk up to the West Hill and sit in the shelter there
> with us two babies and watch the flying bombs coming across the English
> Channel to their destination of major cities. Our mother was not afraid as
> she had endured the London Blitz in 1941 whilst nursing at Knightswood
> Fever Hospital. She felt it far better to see where the planes were going
> rather than being huddled under the table shelter in our little kitchen in
> St George's Road.

Annette was born when the last doodlebugs were flying over and was
nicknamed by her grandmother 'Doodlebug Annie'.[31]

On 21 June, at 8.42 a.m., another doodlebug crashed down to earth on Mayfield Farm, Crowhurst Road, destroying a plant and cattle shed, and seriously injuring one person.[32] Over the following few days, six more flying bombs caused much damage and injury,[33] but no fatalities occurred until 3 July 1944, when 23-year-old Doris Margaret Linch was hit at her home at Spring Cottage in Westfield by a flying bomb and died the next day at the Buchanan Hospital.[34]

M. Desmond Paine remembers school life in the town during the doodle-bug era and the innovative manner in which his school dealt with it:

> Two senior boys sat in the top of the bell tower and watched out to sea. If they saw a doodlebug above the horizon, it would pass over their heads, if below the horizon, it would hit at some point below them, and then they would ring a bell. If they could not see it, it was not necessarily coming near them or was lost in sea-mist. The best they could give even in good weather would be a few seconds warning and we were to duck under our desks. False alarms were accepted as they had little time to think.[35]

On Tuesday 11 July, a number of schoolchildren suffered minor injuries and a school was slightly damaged following the explosion in a nearby orchard of a flying bomb which had been hit by an American fighter. The plane had fired upon the rocket until it plummeted to earth.[36]

Jack Hilder had been on active service with the R.A.F. and had never seen a doodlebug before. On 16 July he was on leave in the *Victoria Inn* on Battle Road when someone shouted that a doodlebug was coming over. Jack raced upstairs to watch the rocket heading towards the pub, before an Allied aircraft flew alongside it and, misguidedly tipping his wing too soon, sent the bomb crashing down into Old Church Road,[37] destroying numbers 17, 19, 21, 23, 25 and 27.[38] Three people were killed and 12 were seriously injured. Among those killed was 43-year-old Home Guard member, Mr William Henry Colbran,[39] who lived at number 25. His daughter and her friend, 15-year-old Brian Bristow, miraculously escaped serious injury as the house collapsed around them. Brian remembers:

> A doodlebug had gone over and the pilot of a fighter plane tipped it and tried to get it away from the built-up area, but unfortunately it came down on us. Mr Colbran, whose house it was, lost his life. He must have been in close vicinity to me, I was just fortunate to get out. It seemed like I was buried for a long time, but I can't remember how long it was. The ambulance lads got me out and took me to hospital; but the thing I do remember, though, is I couldn't hear for some hours after. It hadn't perforated my ear drum but the blast being so close affected my hearing. I can remember my dear dad coming into the hospital and he didn't know I was a casualty. As he had a petrol allowance for his work, he was bringing casualties from somewhere else and he comes into the ward and I tugged his coat. I can't describe his look. I was in hospital for no more than a fortnight. They treated me for

74   *Collapsed houses in Old Church Road after 16 July 1944 bombing.*

shock and bruises. While I was in the Buchanan [Hospital], a bomb came
down on the ward between myself and the patient next to me who was a
fighter pilot. Fortunately for us, it ricocheted off the roof and just the ceiling
came down on our beds: I thought they were after me![40]

Eileen Parish recalls that her friend, home on leave from the Forces,
had heard that an incident had occurred in Old Church Road, and dashed
round to discover that her parents, Frederick Spencer and Martha May
Thompsett, had both been killed in 21 Old Church Road.[41] The Civil
Defence Service went swiftly into action and within an hour of the explosion
had extricated their bodies.[42] Additional help came from the menfolk of
Hollington Methodist Church. Brenda Wallis remembers that night:

> Our minister, Pastor Edwards, said, 'Its no good trying to have a service tonight, we'll do more good by going up and seeing what we can do to help,' so he, my father and various other men of the church went up to Old Church Road and helped with the digging to get people out.[43]

A doodlebug which had been successfully shot down by one of the A.A. batteries in the town crash-landed at Shear Barn Farm in Barley Lane at 7.25 a.m. on 20 July, killing the occupant, Miss Ethel Maria Barnes, who has the unfortunate distinction of being the last person in the borough to die as a result of enemy action.[44]

Although there can be no doubt about just how highly successful and necessary the A.A. gun batteries in the town were, and the sterling work they performed in guarding the town, errors were sometimes made and Allied aircraft mistakenly shot down. John Bristow recalls one such incident in the town involving American Mustang aeroplanes:

> I was in Falaise Road, just going over the brow of the hill with my dad in his car, and to our right was the big battery of anti-aircraft guns on The Oval. As we went over the brow of the hill the guns opened up and I suddenly saw this plane take a direct hit on his nose. Two aircraft had been flying wingtip-to-wingtip, and I recognised them but they thought it was a doodlebug. They had a direct hit on one and it went down into the sea; the other one flew directly over me.[45]

Although deaths caused by enemy action had ceased, the destruction wrought upon the town continued unabated. St Leonards Parish Church suffered a direct hit by a doodlebug which flew in just above sea-level and crashed into the steps of the church at 11.40 p.m. on 29 July 1944, razing the building to the ground and causing damage to two neighbouring houses. One person was seriously injured in the attack.[46] Cecilie Warren recalls the day after the attack on the church, going there to retrieve hymn books from the ruins and seeing 'a lot of debris everywhere and piles of rubble'.[47] The church was later rebuilt, with assistance in its construction from German prisoners of war who were incarcerated near the town.

75 *The last person to die from enemy action in Hastings: Ethel Maria Barnes.*

On Wednesday 2 August 1944, Mayor Dr W.E. Jameson, Deputy Mayor
Councillor F.T. Hussey and the Town Clerk, Mr D.W. Jackson, plus other
dignitaries visited two of the five A.A. batteries which had been used so
effectively in bringing down doodlebugs on their way to London before
they could wreak havoc. The visitors were shown the plotting equipment,
gun batteries and predictor apparatus used in the tracking and downing of
the V1s. The mixed batteries were staffed by the A.T.S and were situated
on the Oval, the West Hill and the East Hill.[48] As was widely known at the
time by locals, one of the staff on the West Hill Battery was Miss Mary
Churchill (now the Lady Soames, D.B.E.), the Prime Minister's daughter,
who was with 481 heavy mixed A.A. Battery R.A., billeted at 27 Priory
Road with Mrs Stone.[49] Lady Soames recalls: 'We were stationed on the
West Hill and the Command Post was in the converted ladies' lavatory on
the hill, which caused much amusement – and sometimes frustration!'[50]
Coincidentally, on the same day as the civic visit to the A.A. batteries, the
15th and final doodlebug attack on the town was at 12.55 p.m. in Battle
Road, causing damage but no loss of life.[51]

76   *St Leonards Parish Church after doodlebug hit 29 July 1944.*

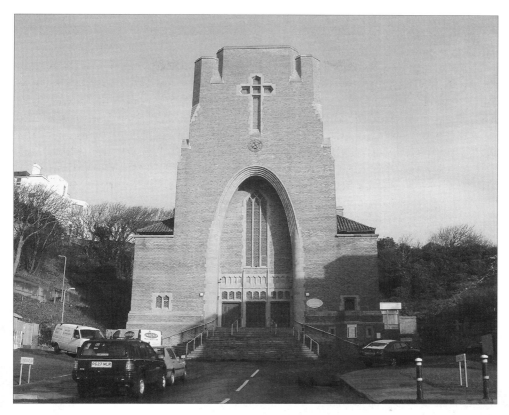

77 *St Leonards Parish Church, 2004.*

In all, 5,000 houses were damaged (17 of which were, or were required to be, demolished), four people lost their lives and 120 people were injured in just 12 weeks by the 15 V1s which came down in the borough.[52] Of the 8,000 flying bombs launched against southern England, it is estimated that at least 3,500 were brought down in Kent and Sussex. By far the greatest number were shot down over the Ashford area, with Battle and Tunbridge Wells competing for second place. At a Battle District Council meeting on Friday 8 September, it was estimated that 412 doodlebugs were shot down within its boundaries, damaging 94 farms in the area.[53]

Bank Holiday Monday 7 August 1944 was one of the quietest on record, a large number of holidaymakers and visitors steering clear of the war-torn town altogether, despite the fact that many other resorts, including some in previously banned areas, were thronging with visitors.[54] However, the outlook brightened when on 25 August 1944 the War Office lifted the five-month coastal ban placed on the town.[55] This action came as military successes in Europe followed one another and the promise of victory drew ever closer. The curfew, which had been in place since 1940, had been abolished,

78   *Hastings beach after reopening on 29 August 1944.*

too. It was a widely held perception among townsfolk that war was coming
to an end; the only question was when the end would come. On Tuesday
29 August, a section of Hastings beach stretching 500-600 yards from the
pier towards Warrior Square was reopened to the public, and the crowds
took advantage of a combination of this and the hot weather, residents and
visitors packing onto it.[56]

Council workers busied themselves repairing lamps and bulbs around the
town ready for the end of the blackout. One large street lamp in Bohemia
Road, outside Park Road Methodist Church, 'switched itself on', bathing
the area in light which had not been seen since 1939. Many locals were
captivated by the glow; one mother even brought her young children, who
had never seen street lamps lit before, to see the spectacle. Then, just
as suddenly, two members of the Electricity Department switched it off
again, sending the street back into the darkness to which it had become
accustomed.

The resurgence in the number of summer visitors continued unabated,
as people flocked to the town in numbers unseen in the past four years.
Finally, the town was returning to its former glory days. Further sections of
the beach were opened in the following week, before the whole promenade
was quickly and efficiently cleared of barbed wire and other anti-landing
devices in mid-September by council workers.[57] An edition of *The Times* from

Thursday 21 September talks of war-scarred Hastings reliving the pre-war days of 'Happy Hastings':

> Here in Hastings a change is coming over the scene, road blocks are being removed, barbed wire is in the process of disappearing, visitors are beginning to pay fleeting visits, bathing has revived and 'Bottle Alley' is beginning to look itself again. But the ravages of war are seen on every hand, and the task of rehabilitation is enough to daunt the stoutest heart.

The paper added that the Borough Engineer estimated that it would take between two and three years to restore the town to its pre-war state.[58]

Many Hastings residents who had been evacuated began returning to the town, only to discover that they were faced with severe difficulties. Among the problems were a loss of personal possessions, a lack of houses to rent, and an increase in rental charges. The Citizens' Advice Bureau told people who had no accommodation to stay away until more houses became available.[59] Otherwise, the town began trying to get back to the normality it had enjoyed before the outbreak of war.

Total blackout was lifted to half-lighting on Sunday 17 September, although at this stage street lighting was still not employed. The Chief Constable of Sussex had this to say on the subject:

> Throughout Sussex it will be permissible to replace blackout by 'half-light'. Complete obscuration of light issuing from buildings will no longer be required provided that the light is diffused by curtains or blinds of any colour or any material, other than the flimsiest, or by any other method giving an equivalent effect.[60]

An issue of much controversy throughout the war was the subject of the evacuation of Hastings Grammar School, which was mentioned sporadically throughout the duration. In a move to appease those opposed to the continued evacuation, from Tuesday 26 September 1944 the new intake of the school were to be taught in Hastings. However, the evacuation of the rest of the school remained in place, despite the fact that many other local schools had restarted back in the town.[61] A condition of schools being allowed back was that adequate bomb shelter would be provided for all pupils. Joyce Wedge remembers sitting in the Silverhill Junior School air-raid shelter during raids, being read stories written by their teacher and children's author, Mrs E.E. Ellsworth:

> Friday afternoon we had a story to finish off the week; the one that was by far the favourite was 'A Highwayman Came Riding'. She would read us a chapter as she wrote it, and we kids were always asking her for the next chapter. It was far better than doing our times tables, or mental arithmetic, or spelling tests! When it was published, my mother bought me a copy, I think it cost all of two shillings and sixpence, and she dated it 3/4/1944. I have fond memories of Mrs E.E. Ellsworth.[62]

The final air-raid alert sounded in the town at 7.15 p.m. on Thursday 9 November 1944 and lasted for 25 minutes. Thereafter the town rejoiced in its silence.[63] Other reactions to the political situation, which gave cause for delight, came about when, after four years, St Clements Caves was closed as a public shelter, to open once again as a visitor attraction the following year if it could be reverted to its former use in time for the summer season. This came despite letters of complaint at the closure being received by the Town Clerk from some elderly and infirm residents, who sought refuge in the caves and were understandably comforted by the second-to-none total protection it offered. Sandbags were also removed from around the streets and there was a marked reduction in the A.R.P. service throughout the town.[64]

On 3 December 1944 over 500 members of the 23rd Battalion Sussex Home Guard mustered at Hastings to officially stand down. Hundreds of onlookers gathered in the streets to watch the Home Guard's last parade.[65] Although the war had not officially ended, this significant step ended the year on a positive note, signalling that Christmas 1944 would, for most people, be the happiest and quietest Christmas for many years.

Seven

A Brighter Future, 1945-1946

The year 1945 began as quietly as the previous year had ended, but with a hint that it would bring the peace for which the town and nation so desperately yearned. In February, the R.O.C. were congratulated for their dedicated work during the tough years of the war, and tribute was paid to them for the time when they were relied upon as the eyes and ears of the R.A.F., straining to detect the first enemy aircraft during the Battle of Britain, the Blitz, the tip-and-run raids and the doodlebugs. Councillor Burgess had this to say of the work of the R.O.C.:

> What this has meant in lives saved by the timely warning of approaching enemy aircraft it is impossible to say, but it must have been enormous ... Men of Observer Corps, we salute you and your devotion to duty. You belong to 'the selected few' but your efforts have saved 'the many'. We offer you our grateful thanks.[1]

Hastings Corporation hurried through assistance to the town's 80 surviving hotels and boarding houses, attempting to lure back the essential Easter visitors to the battered and beleaguered town, although many hotels were still under military requisition, accommodating the vast numbers of Canadian and American troops stationed in the town. Good-humoured posters were drawn up which made light of recent events, exclaiming 'Hastings is ready for your invasion!'[2] By Easter, all of the available hotels and boarding houses in the town were filled to capacity. This came despite a warning from the ex-mayor, Councillor E.M. Ford, that visitors should resist visiting previously banned coastal towns, including Hastings, as they were largely derelict, with only five per cent of the accommodation available in 1939. The story was splashed over the pages of the national newspapers, making many residents wonder as to why the corporation would spend money on getting visitors to the town on the one hand, only to have it nullified by a member of the council on the other. Still, Easter was a great success for Hastings, bringing in countless day trippers and holidaymakers, helping to rebuild the vital tourism industry upon which the town had always relied.[3]

79 *The hostilities are over: V.E. Day in the ruins of St Leonards Parish Church.*

The United States of America was saddened when, on 12 April 1945, only weeks before Allied victory would be assured, President Franklin D. Roosevelt, the man who had led the country through war, died. The Hastings mayor, Alderman A. Blackman, paid this tribute to the late American President:

> By the tragic news this morning of the death of Mr Roosevelt we feel stunned. It is a great disaster to us, for he was the outstanding friend of Britain. A sincere lover of peace, he worked hard to dissipate the war clouds gathering in Europe. His appeals to Germany unheeded, he faced a stupendous task – the conversion of his mighty nation, in a country 7,000 miles long and of diverse creeds and politics, to his conviction of a peril which he foresaw threatened to submerge the whole world ... He knew there was no time to lose. Hitler's gigantic preparations for world domination must be countered by America's vast resources and the will of a unified people.[4]

As V.E. Day loomed, the town prepared for the ensuing celebrations with exceptional rigour. Traders were advised in the 5 May edition of the local newspaper that when V.E. Day came they were to remain open for one hour following the announcement, then close for the remainder of the day and the following day. Dairymen were requested to deliver on both V.E. Day and the following day, and bakers were asked to keep deliveries as much the same as possible and to open the day after V.E. Day for the sale of bread only. The town and country was, in the build-up to V.E. Day, buzzing with excitement that victory was imminent, the exact day and hour the only question remaining. Pubs, hotels, clubs and entertainment venues in the borough were all given special licences to remain open for an extra hour on V.E. Day.

After almost six of the most momentous years to have been experienced in the borough, the news that victory had been secured was received over the wireless at 3 p.m. by the Prime Minister, and hostilities in Europe were finally over. Churchill announced to an expectant country: 'German armed forces surrendered unconditionally on May 7th. Hostilities in Europe ended officially at midnight, May 8th 1945.'[5] The Town Council listened intently to the Prime Minister's broadcast and within an hour, at 4 p.m., the mayor, Alderman A. Blackman, spoke to a huge, relieved and joyous crowd from the balcony of the Town Hall, greeted by cheers and applause. He said:

> To my fellow citizens – we have reached the end of organised war in Europe. The end of a nightmare – the end for which so many have worked so hard. Nations united under the banner of freedom and liberty have triumphed. We can rejoice, but let us not forget in our rejoicing and thanksgiving those who have loved ones still fighting in the Far East and think also with deep sympathy of the bereaved.

Three cheers for victory were called for, to which the gathered crowds gave a hearty response.

Joyce Wedge was at the High School, assembled for their Speech Day at the White Rock Theatre, when the announcement came through:

> Mary Churchill was the VIP giving out the prizes, some boys from the High School were in the balcony and we girls were seated downstairs on either side with our mothers in the middle in front of the stage. Everyone had been listening to the radio, and when my mother came in, she gave her head a little shake: it wasn't over yet! Then part way through the proceedings a man appears through the back curtain, and hands a note to one of the dignitaries. The announcement was made that the war was over and there was uproar! We were given a holiday there and then. Later there were celebrations in Alexandra Park with music, dancing, and lights – after all the blackout, it seemed wonderful to us youngsters.[6]

80 *The V.E. Day crowds at Winkle Island.*

Celebratory flags soon appeared on the town's hotels, pubs, shops, public buildings and private homes. Firemen worked to run flags through the town centre and over the Memorial in time for the dozens of street parties held all around. Instead of the wailing air-raid siren, church bells pealed all over the town, the sound of which people must have been grateful to hear, having been denied it for so long. Patriotic residents paraded the streets decked out in red, white and blue costumes. Ken Jones was one of hundreds of people celebrating the momentous occasion at the Memorial in the town centre. He recalls much joyous and rapturous singing and dancing going on there for most of that night.[7]

Many St Leonards residents, regardless of religious denomination, followed a long procession led by the Hastings Citadel Salvation Army to the symbolic ruins of St Leonards Parish Church for a service of thanksgiving for victory and of remembrance for all those who gave their lives fighting for peace. The service must have been a highly emotive one, with every resident of the town touched in some way by the loss of a friend or relative in the struggle. Later that night, at 11.40 p.m., 100 people stood in the ruins to observe two minutes' silence in remembrance, of that time on the 27 July 1944, when the church was all but flattened by the flying bomb.

In the Old Town, Winkle Island saw more locals partaking in revelries than on the busiest of summer days. M. Desmond Paine recalls that unlimited roast potatoes and beer were on offer at this party.[8] Perhaps the supply of beer would explain Derek Marsh's strongest recollection from the evening, when he witnessed an American sergeant, 'drunk as a lord', picking up his motorbike and climbing on, then falling off the other side, and repeating

81 *V.E. Day celebrations in Clarence Road.*

82 *West Hill V.E. Day celebrations.*

the process over and over before finally giving up any idea of riding to wherever he thought he needed to go, and sinking another pint.[9]

On V.E. Night, exuberant dances, private parties and street parties were held all over the town. Joan Fincham recalls one such joyous party on Boyne Road: 'We had a party in the street organised by the mums. How they managed it, I do not know, but somehow there was a great spread of goodies for all us children.'[10] The celebratory mood around the entire country was electric, with almost every resident taking part in some festivity or another.

On the West Hill a large celebratory dance took place, which Terry Breeds, the girl who later became his wife, and a dozen friends attended:

> The evening on the West Hill was fantastic. They had fireworks, a band for outdoor dancing, and a large bonfire that was probably part of a series around the coast. I don't know what time it all ended – it was still going on when I left, and to be quite honest I think the atmosphere lasted for a lot longer than one day. It was great, although the war in the Far East was still going on, which I suppose tempered things down a bit.[11]

More good news arrived on Friday 11 May, when the lighting restriction was lifted throughout the country, officially ending the blackout. Right across the borough, people were able to take down heavy curtains, chip off black paint and peel back the anti-glass-splinter tape from the windows.[12]

83   *Norman Dengate in 1944.*

Celebrations continued throughout the week, and on Sunday 13 May a mile-long parade walked from the Memorial to Alexandra Park, which was filled with an amazing 10,000 people, all gathered in a united service of thanksgiving for victory and peace in Europe. It began with the singing of the National Anthem, and was then declared open by the Mayor of Hastings. All of the services who had provided the town with their indispensable help during the bleakest of times, were represented at the park, proudly marching in their uniforms behind bands and flags, themselves undoubtedly relieved that their role had become ceremonial.[13]

A step towards rehabilitation came when the popular bathing pool reopened for business on 19 May; it had been closed down on 3 September 1939 when it was requisitioned by the military and Civil Defence. The baths were immediately filled and quickly returned to their pre-war function as one of the town's leading leisure attractions.[14] As more and more residents returned to the town, so more and more businesses began to reopen. The military derequisitioned further hotels, as many of the billeted troops were no longer required for warfare in Europe; many were sent out to assist in the Far East, where the war continued to rage. The town's largest hotel, the *Queen's Hotel*, however, continued to be held by the military, much to the dismay of the hotel's owner, Jack Humphries, who lamented that:

> We are getting between 30 and 40 letters a day from people writing to book rooms because they say they have heard that the hotel has been freed. It is very evident that a lot of visitors want to come to Hastings again, and we should like to be able to accommodate some of them.[15]

The *Queen's Hotel* was in fact derequisitioned twice, and it was perhaps the first occasion, which lasted only days before the hotel was sharply requisitioned once more, which sparked rumours that it would be available for holidaymakers. The extensive removals on both occasions was undertaken by Dengate's furniture firm. Cousins Norman and Gordon Dengate both assisted in the process. Norman remembers that a complex numbering system was used to mark the furniture from each hotel room, since it had to be placed back exactly where it had come from. Both Norman and Gordon recall throwing all the mattresses and bedding used by the military over a balcony into a huge heap, before loading it into trucks to be taken away. The hotel furniture, which had been placed in storage, was then carefully put back into each room so that the hotel could welcome the summer visitors to the town.[16]

Over the coming months, the freedom of the borough was conferred four times. First of all Dr William Ernest Jameson J.P. received the honour for his dedicated and courageous duty as mayor of the town from 1940-4. On receiving the honour, Dr Jameson recalled his feelings at the time when invasion seemed inevitable, and town officials waited anxiously for the 'code word' to be received, although tantalisingly he does not reveal what this was:

> We knew of the massing of the enemy's barges across the narrow seas. The Town Clerk and I awaited with the gravest anxiety the possible receipt of one short word – the code word which would have meant the total evacuation of the remaining population. We should have had an end of civil administration and complete control of all the affairs, not only of our town, but of the whole area by the military.[17]

The second and third conferments of the freedom of the borough were bestowed upon Winston Churchill, who was Lord Warden of the Cinque Ports,[18] and Viscount Montgomery, in recognition of his pre-eminent war service and leadership.[19] The fourth wartime freedom of the borough was conferred upon the Town Clerk at the time, Daniel Wilfred Jackson, who retired in 1946 after 25 years in the job.[20]

After almost six years of coastal darkness, on 15 July 1945, the town's 3,000 street lamps were illuminated to full, peacetime brightness a sight not seen by many small children. The lamps, which would reduce the number of deaths caused by the total darkness, attracted many people keen to take a stroll along the promenade.[21]

After V.E. Day came a bloody and destructive few weeks in the Far East. Day after day, huge quantities of bombs were dropped on Japan. By the end of June, 105.6 square miles of the total 257.2 square miles of Japan's six largest cities were destroyed. At 8.15 a.m. on 6 August 1945, the world's first nuclear device, a 9,000lb bomb called 'Little Boy', was dropped over Hiroshima, causing the widest death and devastation known to man by a single bomb. Between 60,000 and 80,000 people died and 70,000 suffered horrific burn injuries. As if this were not sufficient, just three days later 'Fat Boy' was dropped by the Americans over Nagasaki, killing 35,000, although as Matanle reminds us:

> It should not be forgotten that the real total of killed and injured for both nuclear attacks was very much higher than the figures for immediate

casualties suggest. The subsequent radiation sickness and high incidences
of cancers, congenitally abnormal births, cataract, spontaneous abortion,
and other conditions greatly increased the total casualties over a period of
20 and 30 years.[22]

A combination of the two horrific nuclear attacks and Russia's declaration of war against Japan on 8 August 1945 forced the Japanese to realise
the odds were stacked against them and they could not possibly win the
war. On 15 August 1945 victory was assured in the Far East as Japan
unconditionally surrendered to the Allies: V.J. Day had come at last. In
Britain, the mood of the country was more subdued, perhaps because of
the dreadful way in which peace was achieved, or perhaps because of the
distance from that theatre of war. In Hastings, many parties took place
celebrating the fact that total war was finally over, but with less ceremony
and jubilation than those which marked V.E. Day. Eileen Parish remembers
that she and her mother had differing ideas as to the commemoration
of V.E. and V.J. Days:

> My mother's idea of celebrating was to spring clean the house, cleaning
> the windows, washing the paintwork, washing the curtains and all this sort
> of thing. We were there putting the curtains up at night [V.E. night] and I
> remember seeing all these people going home after being out and having
> a good time and I thought I'm not very keen on this. By the time V.J. Day
> came, I thought blow that, I'm not spring cleaning for this one, so I went
> out and joined the rest of them up Duke Road, dancing in the street.[23]

84   *A brighter future. Hastings seafront in July 1945.*

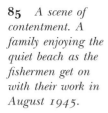

85 *A scene of contentment. A family enjoying the quiet beach as the fishermen get on with their work in August 1945.*

In a marked change, the town was subject to construction rather than destruction, when the Town Council initiated plans for the rebuilding of Hastings. Intended to alleviate the acute housing shortage, this began with the erection of 50 houses in Rock Lane at a cost of £62,000. The Council and Borough Engineer, Sidney Little, also began redevelopment plans for over 1,000 homes in Hollington.[24] In areas such as Emmanuel Road, St Georges Road and Whitefriars Road, demolished houses were cleared and blocks of flats put up in their place. To this day the evidence of just how prolific enemy action was can still be seen all over Hastings, particularly in the more recent buildings disrupting rows of Victorian architecture.

Other changes to affect the town were the gradual clearance of landmines from Fairlight, and of pipe mines from around the Harrow, which had been laid at the height of invasion fears.[25] It was not until January 1948 that a two-mile stretch of coast at Fairlight Cove, including Lovers Seat, was cleared of landmines. According to *The Times*, this left only one small area which still contained landmines and was, therefore, a danger to the public. The problem of mines being washed up on the town's beaches continued for some time after the war had ended, often forcing the temporary closure of sections of the coastline.[26]

The August holiday season got off to a prosperous start with the further opening of accommodation. Forty-four hotels, 145 boarding houses and 447 private houses were made available and were fully booked for the August Bank Holiday, making it the best summer since before the war. Estimates put the amount spent in the town at £150,000 per week, a much needed boost to the local economy. Day trippers poured into the war-scarred town at a rate of 20,000 per day, keen to enjoy the newly reopened leisure and pleasure activities. The boating lake in Alexandra Park opened for the first

86 *In memory of the town's 154 civilian war dead: Hastings War Memorial, Alexandra Park, 2004.*

time since 1939 and St Clements Caves reverted to its former purpose as a visitor attraction, but with a new story added to its already interesting history.[27] For some visitors, it would be the first opportunity to revisit the town since before the outbreak of war. The unavoidable sight of collapsed buildings, bullet-ridden pavements and large holes in Victorian terraces where houses once stood must have been startling. The town bore the scars of 550 H.E. bombs in addition to 762 incendiary devices and 15 flying bombs, which led to 154 civilian deaths, 260 serious injuries and 439 slight injuries.[28] After some of the darkest years in Hastings' history, the town was finally getting back on its feet, and soon surpassing its former heyday of the 1930s.

'On its war record, the Premier Cinque Port has full reason for pride and in looking back over the past years in the front line can feel that it has been steadfast, courageous and worthy of its historic past.' – *Hastings & St Leonards Observer, 12 May 1945*

Notes

Abbreviations used in the footnotes

CWD   Civilian War Dead in the Hastings, Battle, Bexhill, Rye and Rother Regions (1939-45) compiled by the Hastings and Rother Family History Society

ESRO   East Sussex Record Office

HC   Hastings Cemetery

HM   Hastings Museum

HRL   Hastings Reference Library

HSLO   *Hastings & St Leonards Observer*

IWM   Imperial War Museum

TCDR   Town Clerk's Department Records listing bomb incidents

TNA   The National Archives

WCCDR   War Cabinet Civil Defence Report

WDP1   Town Clerk's Department Records form WDP1 – Return as to Damage to Property Directly Consequent upon Bombardment or Attack from the Air

Chapter 1 – In Preparation for War 1938-1939

1   ESRO: A.R.P. Committee DH/B51/1 22 November 1935.

2   ESRO: A.R.P. Committee DH/B51/1 2 December 1937.

3   HSLO 27 March 1937, 5 June 1937, 3 July 1937, 10 July 1937.

4   HSLO 22 January 1938.

5   HSLO 5 February 1938.

6   ESRO: A.R.P. Committee DH/B51/1 24 February 1938.

7   IWM PP/MCR/205 Records of the Hastings Peace Group.

8   HSLO 5 February 1938.

9   TNA HO186/361 WCCDR 5, 18 February 1940.

10   Matanle, I., *World War Two* (1997).

11   HSLO 12 March 1938.

12   ESRO: A.R.P. Committee DH/B51/1 11 October 1938.

13   ESRO: A.R.P. Committee DH/B51/1 26 September 1938.

14   ESRO: A.R.P. Committee DH/B51/1 4 October 1938.

15   ESRO: A.R.P. Committee DH/B51/1 11 October 1938 and HSLO 1 October 1938.

16   Conisbee, L.R., Manwaring Baines, J. and Bygate, N., *The History of Hastings Grammar School* (1966).

17   Letter from M. Desmond Paine, 10 December 2003.

18   Telephone call with Ken Perkins, 26 November 2003.

19   ESRO: A.R.P. Committee DH/B51/1 6 September 1939.

20   HSLO 20 May 1939.

21   ESRO: A.R.P. Committee DH/B51/1 6 February 1939.

22   HSLO 1 July 1939 and 15 July 1939.

23   HSLO 26 August 1939.

24   Email from Olga Walker, 21 June 2004.

25   HSLO 2 September 1939.

26   Telephone call with Marjory Manton B.E.M., 14 March 2004.

27 Interview with Brenda Wallis, 25 June 2004.
28 Letter from Dennis Layell, 8 January 2004.
29 Letter from Patricia Pockett, 30 November 2003.
30 ESRO: A.R.P. Committee DH/B51/2 3 September 1939.
31 Interview with Derek Marsh, 23 August 2003.
32 HSLO 6 January, 13 January, 27 January, 9 March, 22 June 1940.
33 TNA HO186/138 WCCDR 8 September 1939.
34 TNA HO186/356 WCCDR 18 February-3 March.
35 Interview with Brenda Glazier 24 August 2003.
36 Email from Ken Jones, 14 November 2003.
37 Email from Terry Breeds, 17 June 2004.
38 Email from Les Breach, 26 November 2003.
39 Telephone call with Ken Perkins, 26 November 2003.
40 Ramsey, W. (ed.), *The Blitz Then and Now, Vol. 1* (1987).
41 HSLO 15 June 1940.
42 HSLO 13 Jan 1940.
43 Letter from Joan Rider, August 2003.
44 HSLO 6 January 1940.
45 Letter from Dennis Layell, 8 January 2004.

CHAPTER 2 – EVACUATION, THE BATTLE OF BRITAIN AND THE FIRST RAIDS, 1940

1   HSLO 27 January 1940, 3 February 1940, 17 February 1940.
2   TNA HO186/356 WCCDR 5-18 February.
3   HSLO 17 February 1940.
4   IWM 04/2/1 – Lieutenant G.R. Price RNVR, *My War* (1991).
5   HSLO 22 June 1940.
6   HSLO 18 May 1940.
7   HSLO 8 June 1940.
8   TNA HO186/361 WCCDR 9 June 1940-7 July 1940.
9   TNA HO186/361 WCCDR 9 June 1940-7 July 1940.
10 HSLO 18 May 1940.
11 Interview with Brenda Wallis, 25 June 2004.
12 HSLO 25 May 1940.
13 Interview with Iona Muggridge, 1 October 2003.
14 Interview with Carol Boorman, 12 September 2003.
15 Peak, S., *Fishermen of Hastings* (1985).
16 Matanle, I., *World War Two* (1997).
17 HSLO 8 June 1940.
18 www.winstonchurchill.org.
19 Lampe, D., *The Last Ditch* (1968).

20 HSLO 15 June 1940.
21 TNA HO186/361 WCCDR 9 June 1940-7 July 1940.
22 HSLO 22 June 1940.
23 TNA HO186/361 WCCDR 9 June 1940-7 July 1940.
24 HSLO 13 July 1940.
25 HSLO 7 September 1940.
26 TNA HO186/361 WCCDR 4 August 1940.
27 HSLO 13 and 20 July and Conisbee, L.R., Manwaring Baines, J. and Bygate, N., *The History of Hastings Grammar School* (1966).
28 Email from Ken Jones, 14 November 2003.
29 IWM: Misc 194/2863 – Letter from Hastings Education Committee.
30 Conisbee, L.R., Manwaring Baines, J. and Bygate, N., *The History of Hastings Grammar School* (1966).
31 Letter from M. Desmond Paine, 10 December 2003.
32 HSLO 3 August 1940.
33 HSLO 17 August 1940.
34 Interview with Gordon Dengate, 24 September 2003.
35 Telephone call with Peggy Smith, 26 June 2004.
36 Interview with Lew Boorman, 12 September 2003.
37 Email from Ronald Ollington, 27 June 2004.
38 Email from Terry Breeds, 17 June 2004.
39 Armes, D., *Ware to War 1939-1945* (2002).
40 Email from Olga Walker, 21 June 2004.
41 Interview with Maisie Pocock, 17 September 2003.
42 Email from Charles Clark, 22 November 2003.
43 Letter from Joan Fincham, October 2003.
44 Interview with Brenda Glazier, 24 August 2003.
45 HSLO 21 December 1940.
46 Email from Les Breach, 26 November 2003.
47 HM: TCDR.
48 HM: WDP1.
49 Letter from Beryl Latimer, 10 September 2003.
50 Interview with Brenda Hunt, 22 August 2003.
51 *Hastings and St Leonards in the Front Line*, produced by HSLO (1945), and Violet Gooday's obituary, HSLO August 1940.
52 HSLO 3 and 10 August 1940.
53 TNA AIR 25/197 – No.11 Group Operation Instruction number 14 autumn 1940.
54 TNA CAB/146/6.
55 HSLO 2 June 1945.
56 Angell, S., *The Secret Sussex Resistance* (1996).

57 Interview with Iona Muggridge, 1 October 2003.
58 Interview with Lew Boorman, 12 September 2003.
59 Interview with Margaret Humphrey, 24 September 2003.
60 HM: TCDR.
61 Caroline Frances Felton's obituary HSLO, 24 August 1940 and CWD.
62 HM: TCDR and *Hastings and St Leonards in the Front Line* (1945).
63 Mace, M.F., *They also Served – The Story of Sussex Lifeboats at War* (2001).
64 *The Times*, 30 August 1943.
65 Email from Frank Gutsell, 3 December 2003.
66 Interview with Eileen Parish, 8 August 2003.
67 Interview with Brenda Walllis, 25 June 2004.
68 HM: WDP1.
69 HM: TCDR.
70 HM: TCDR and *Hastings and St Leonards in the Front Line* (1945).
71 HRL: A.R.P. Logbook 1940/1941.
72 Rowland, D., *Spitfires over Sussex* (2000).
73 HSLO 31 August 1940.
74 Interview with John Bristow, 25 July 2003 and interview with Jack Hilder, 6 August 2003.
75 Letter from Dorothy Wellings, 26 November 2003.
76 HSLO 31 August, 7 September, 14 September, 21 September, 28 September, 5 October, 12 October, 26 October, 16 November 1940.
77 HSLO 21 September 1940.
78 HM: TCDR.
79 HM: Samaritan Service: Persons rendered homeless.
80 HM: TCDR.
81 HRL: A.R.P. Logbook 1940/1941.
82 Ramsey, W. (ed.), *The Blitz Then and Now, Vol. 2.* (1988).
83 HSLO 28 September 1940.
84 German War Dead: http://www.volksbund. de/graebersuche/content_suche.asp.
85 Interview with Jack Hilder, 6 August 2003.
86 HC burial records.
87 HM: WDP1.
88 HM: TCDR.
89 Letter from Joan Rider, August 2003.
90 Interview with Lew Boorman, 12 September 2003.
91 HRL: A.R.P. Logbook 1940/1941.
92 Mace, M.F., *They also Served – The Story of Sussex Lifeboats at War* (2001).
93 HM: A.R.P. Log Book.
94 HM: A.R.P. Log Book.
95 HM: TCDR.
96 HM: WDP1.
97 HM: WDP1 and *Hastings and St Leonards in the Front Line* (1945).
98 CWD; interview with Eveline Edwards, 4 August 2003.
99 Interview with Brenda Glazier, 24 August 2003.
100 Interview with Hilda Marden, 17 October 2003.
101 *Hastings and St Leonards in the Front Line* (1945) and HSLO 5 October 1940.
102 HM: TCDR.
103 HSLO 25 July 1936.
104 HC burial records.
105 Interview with Brenda Wallis, 25 June 2004.
106 Interview with Norman Dengate, 19 August 2003.
107 Letter from Joan Rider, August 2003.
108 HM: A.R.P. Log Book.
109 TNA HO186/365, WCCDR 2 September- 29 September 1940.
110 HM: A.R.P. Log Book.
111 HM: TCDR.
112 HM: WDP1.
113 Interview with Iona Muggridge, 1 October 2003.
114 HM: WDP1.
115 HM: TCDR.
116 CWD; interview with Eveline Edwards, 4 August 2003.
117 HM: TCDR.
118 HM: TCDR and HM: WDP1.
119 HSLO 12 October 1940.
120 CWD.
121 HSLO 26 October 1940.
122 HSLO 12 October 1940.
123 HM: TCDR and *Hastings and St Leonards in the Front Line* (1945).
124 HM: WDP1.
125 HM: TCDR.
126 Interview with Eileen Parish, 8 August 2003.
127 *Hastings and St Leonards in the Front Line* (1945).
128 HSLO 26 October 1940.
129 HSLO 2 and 16 November 1940.
130 Interview with Iona Muggridge, 1 October 2003.
131 Email from Les Breach, 26 November 2003.
132 HM: WDP1 and HM: TCDR.
133 ESRO: A.R.P. Committee DH/B51/2 17 October 1940.
134 *Hastings and St Leonards in the Front Line* (1945).

135 Interview with Brenda Glazier, 24 August
      2003.
136 Interview with Carol Boorman,
      12 September 2003.
137 Email from Les Breach, 26 November
      2003.
138 Interview with Derek Marsh, 23 August
      2003.
139 HSLO 1 March 1941.
140 ESRO: A.R.P. Committee DH/B51/2
      24 April 1941.
141 HRL: A.R.P. Logbook 1940/1941.
142 Goss, C., *Luftwaffe Fighter-Bombers over Britain*
      (2003).

CHAPTER 3 – NIGHT RAIDS, 1941

1   HSLO 4 January 1941.
2   HSLO 4 January 1941.
3   HSLO 11 January 1941.
4   Interview with Sheila Dengate,
     24 September 2003.
5   HSLO 8 February 1941.
6   Interview with Norman Dengate, 19 August
     2003.
7   Interview with Iona Muggridge, 1 October
     2003.
8   HRL: A.R.P. Logbook 1940/1941.
9   HM: TCDR.
10 HSLO 1 February 1941.
11 HSLO 18 January 1941.
12 HM: WDP1 and HM: TCDR.
13 HSLO 22 March 1941.
14 Interview with Eveline Edwards, 4 August
     2003.
15 Interview with Eileen Parish, 8 August
     2003.
16 Interview with Joyce Dengate, 19 August
     2003.
17 Email from Derek Hutchinson,
     15 November 2003.
18 Email from Cecilie Warren, 17 June 2004.
19 HSLO 1 February 1941.
20 HSLO 24 May 1941.
21 Email from Ken Perkins, 26 June 2004.
22 HSLO 8 March 1941.
23 ESRO: A.R.P. Committee DH/B51/2
     24 March 1941.
24 ESRO: A.R.P. Committee DH/B51/2
     17 March 1941.
25 ESRO: A.R.P. Committee DH/B51/2
     2 June 1941.
26 Interview with Joyce Dengate, 19 August
     2003.
27 Interview with Brenda Glazier, 24 August
     2003.
28 Email from Frank Gutsell, 3 December
     2003.
29 HM: TCDR.

30 HM: WDP1.
31 HM: Samaritan Service record book,
     8 April 1941.
32 HSLO 12 April 1941 and *Hastings and
     St Leonards in the Front Line* (1945).
33 HSLO 12 April 1941.
34 HM: TCDR.
35 HSLO 14 June 1941.
36 HSLO 28 June and 5 July 1941.
37 HSLO 8 November 1941.
38 HM: Letters and confidential files 1941
     and 1942.
39 HM: WDP1.
40 Matanle, I., *World War Two* (1997).
41 HSLO 5 December 1942.

CHAPTER 4 – TIP-AND-RUN RAIDS, 1942

1   HSLO 10 January 1942 and *Hastings and
     in the Front Line* (1945).
2   HM: Triumvirate meeting minutes,
     24 March 1942.
3   HSLO 17 January 1942.
4   HSLO 24 January and 18 April 1942.
5   HSLO 25 April 1942 and *Hastings and
     St Leonards in the Front Line* (1945).
6   HM: WDP1.
7   HM: TCDR and HSLO 9 May 1942.
8   HSLO 9 May 1942.
9   Caroline Harmer and Sarah Ann Cox's
     obituary, HSLO 16 May 1942.
10 James and Mary Gamblen's obituary, HSLO
     9 May 1942 and CWD.
11 HM: TCDR.
12 HM: WDP1.
13 Interview with Derek Marsh, 23 August
     2003.
14 TNA AIR 25/206 Air Ministry account
     1943.
15 HSLO 23 May 1942; CWD.
16 HSLO 23 May 1942.
17 HM: WDP1.
18 HSLO 23 May 1942.
19 Burgess, P. and Saunders, A., *Blitz over
     Sussex 1941-1942* (1994).
20 Hawkinge Cemetery records.
21 HM: Triumvirate meeting minutes,
     24 March 1942.
22 HM: List of personnel retained in the
     event of evacuation 28 March 1942.
23 HM: A.R.P. Exercise 20 June 1942.
24 HSLO 27 June 1942.
25 HSLO 29 August 1942.
26 HM: WDP1.
27 Letter from Joan Fincham, October 2003.
28 HM: WDP1, HSLO 26 September 1942
     and 23 May 1942 and CWD.
29 Interview with Gordon Dengate,
     24 September 2003.

30 *Hastings and St Leonards in the Front Line* (1945).
31 CWD.
32 Goss, C., *Luftwaffe Fighter-Bombers over Britain* (2003).
33 HSLO 16 January 1943.
34 *Hastings and St Leonards in the Front Line* (1945).
35 HM: TCDR.
36 *Hastings and St Leonards in the Front Line* (1945) and CWD.
37 HSLO 12 December 1942.
38 *Hastings and St Leonards in the Front Line* (1945) and CWD.
39 HSLO 2 January 1943.

CHAPTER 5 – THE WORST ATTACKS, 1943

1   HSLO 9 January 1943.
2   TNA AIR 25/205 Air Ministry account 1943.
3   Hawkinge Cemetery records.
4   Burgess, P. and Saunders, A., *Bombers over Sussex 1943-1945* (1995).
5   TNA AIR 25/205 Air Ministry account 1943.
6   Hawkinge Cemetery records.
7   HSLO 16 January 1943 and HM: TCDR.
8   HM: WDP1.
9   *Hastings and St Leonards in the Front Line* (1945).
10 HSLO 30 January 1943.
11 HM: WDP1.
12 *Hastings and St Leonards in the Front Line* (1945).
13 CWD.
14 TNA: AIR 25/205 Air Ministry account 1943 and HSLO 13 March 1943.
15 Goss, C., *Luftwaffe Fighter-Bombers over Britain* (2003).
16 *Hastings and St Leonards in the Front Line* (1945) and HSLO 13 March 1943.
17 HM: WDP1.
18 Interview with Eileen Parish, 8 August 2003.
19 *Hastings and St Leonards in the Front Line* (1945) and HSLO 13 March 1943.
20 Interview with Eileen Parish, 8 August 2003.
21 Interview with Brenda Glazier, 24 August 2003.
22 Interview with John Bristow, 25 July 2003.
23 Interview with Brenda Wallis, 25 June 2004.
24 Emma Riggs Hoad's obituary, HSLO 20 March 1943.
25 CWD.
26 Emma Louisa Giles' obituary, HSLO 20 March 1943.

27 HSLO 20 March 1943.
28 HSLO 1 May 1943.
29 Peak, S., *Fishermen of Hastings* (1985).
30 Interview with Iona Muggridge, 1 October 2003.
31 TNA: AIR 25/205 Air Ministry account 1943 and HSLO 29 May 1943.
32 HM: TCDR.
33 CWD.
34 Albert Henry Reader's obituary, HSLO 29 May 1943.
35 HSLO 29 May 1943.
36 Goss, C., *Luftwaffe Fighter-Bombers over Britain* (2003).
37 Interview with John Bristow, 25 July 2003.
38 Goss, C., *Luftwaffe Fighter-Bombers over Britain* (2003).
39 TNA: AIR 25/206 Air Ministry account 1943.
40 HM: TCDR.
41 TNA: AIR 25/206 Air Ministry account 1943.
42 HSLO 1 May, 12 June and 14 August 1943.
43 *The Times*, 30 August 1943.
44 Interview with Eileen Parish, 8 August 2003.
45 HSLO 11 September 1943.
46 TNA: AIR 25/207 Air Ministry account 1943.
47 *Bexhill Observer*, 23 October 1943.
48 Interview with June Kemp, 24 September 2003.
49 HM: TCDR.

CHAPTER 6 – THE FINAL RAIDS, D-DAY AND THE DOODLEBUG ERA, 1944

1   HM: WDP1 and HM: TCDR.
2   HM: TCDR.
3   HM: WDP1 and CWD.
4   HSLO 18 March 1944 and 15 February 1941.
5   HM: WDP1.
6   HSLO 18 March 1944.
7   ESRO: A.R.P. Committee DH/B51/2 21 March 1944.
8   HM: WDP1 and HM: TCDR.
9   Burgess, P. and Saunders, A., *Bombers over Sussex 1943-1945* (1995).
10 HSLO 29 January 1944.
11 Burgess, P. and Saunders, A., *Bombers over Sussex 1943-1945* (1995).
12 HSLO 25 March 1944.
13 HSLO 24 June 1944.
14 HSLO 12 May 1945.
15 Interview with June Kemp, 24 September 2003.
16 Interview with Iona Muggridge, 1 October 2003.

17 Interview with Gordon Dengate,
    24 September 2003.
18 Letter from Joan Fincham, October 2003.
19 Matanle, I., *World War Two* (1997).
20 Ogly, B., *Doodlebugs and Rockets* (1992).
21 *The Times*, 9 September 1944.
22 Interview with Bob Gearing, 9 October
    2003.
23 Ogly, B., *Doodlebugs and Rockets* (1992).
24 HM: TCDR and *Hastings and St Leonards in
    the Front Line* (1945).
25 *Hastings and St Leonards in the Front Line*
    (1945).
26 Interview with Bob Gearing, 9 October
    2003.
27 Email from Joyce Wedge, 20 November
    2003.
28 Interviews with Eileen Parish, 8 August
    2003, Jack Hilder, 6 August 2003, Bob
    Gearing, 9 October 2003 and Lew
    Boorman, 12 September 2003.
29 *The Times*, 9 September 1944.
30 Interview with Gordon Dengate,
    24 September 2003.
31 Letter from Annie and Cathleen Munn,
    3 August 2003.
32 HM: TCDR and *Hastings and St Leonards in
    the Front Line* (1945).
33 HM: WDP1 and HM: TCDR.
34 HM: TCDR and HSLO 15 July 1944.
35 Letter from M. Desmond Paine,
    10 December 2003.
36 HSLO 15 July 1944.
37 Interview with Jack Hilder, 6 August 2003.
38 HM: WDP1 and HM: TCDR.
39 HSLO 22 July 1944 CWD.
40 Interview with Brian Bristow, 5 August
    2003.
41 Interview with Eileen Parish, 8 August
    2003.
42 HSLO 22 July 1944.
43 Interview with Brenda Wallis, 25 June
    2004.
44 HM: WDP1 and HM: TCDR.
45 Interview with John Bristow, 25 July 2003.
46 HM: TCDR and *Hastings and St Leonards in
    the Front Line* (1945).
47 Email from Cecilie Warren, 17 June 2004.
48 HSLO 5 August 1944.
49 HSLO 9 November 1946.
50 Letter from The Lady Soames D.B.E.,
    29 July 2003.
51 HM: TCDR.
52 HSLO 16 September 1944.
53 *The Times*, 9 September 1944.
54 HSLO 12 August 1944.

55 HSLO 26 August 1944.
56 HSLO 2 September 1944.
57 HSLO 23 September 1944 and 14 October
    1944.
58 *The Times*, 21 September 1944.
59 HSLO 23 September 1944.
60 HSLO 16 September 1944.
61 HSLO 2 and 16 September.
62 Email from Joyce Wedge, 20 November
    2003.
63 *Hastings and St Leonards in the Front Line*
    (1945).
64 ESRO: A.R.P. Committee DH/B51/2
    21 November 1944.
65 HSLO 9 December 1944.

**CHAPTER 7 – A BRIGHTER FUTURE,
1945-1946**

1   HSLO 3 February 1945.
2   HSLO 10 February 1945.
3   HSLO 31 March 1945.
4   HSLO 14 April 1945.
5   www.winstonchurchill.org.
6   Email from Joyce Wedge, 25 November
    2003.
7   Email from Ken Jones, 14 November
    2003.
8   Letter from M. Desmond Paine,
    10 December 2003.
9   Interview with Derek Marsh, 23 August
    2003.
10 Letter from Joan Fincham, October 2003.
11 Email from Terry Breeds, 18 June 2004.
12 HSLO 12 May 1945.
13 HSLO 12 and 19 May 1945.
14 HSLO 19 May 1945.
15 HSLO 23 June 1945.
16 Interviews with Norman Dengate, 19
    August 2003, and Gordon Dengate, 24
    September 2003.
17 HSLO 9 June 1945.
18 HSLO 15 December 1945.
19 HSLO 9 March 1946.
20 *The Times*, 9 May 1946.
21 HSLO 21 July 1945.
22 Matanle, I., *World War Two* (1997).
23 Interview with Eileen Parish, 8 August
    2003.
24 HSLO 22 September 1945 and 11 July
    1946.
25 HSLO 19 January 1946.
26 *The Times*, 20 January 1948, 10 January
    1946 and 29 December 1945.
27 HSLO 4 and 11 August 1945.
28 *Hastings and St Leonards in the Front Line*
    (1945).

BIBLIOGRAPHY

Angell, S., *The Secret Sussex Resistance* (1996)

Armes, D., *Ware to War 1939-1945* (2002)

Burgess, P. and Saunders, A., *Battle over Sussex 1940* (2003)

Burgess, P. and Saunders, A., *Blitz over Sussex 1941-1942* (1994)

Burgess, P. and Saunders, A., *Bombers over Sussex 1943-1945* (1995)

Conisbee, L.R., Manwaring Baines, J. and Bygate, N., *The History of Hastings Grammar School* (1966)

Goss, C., *Luftwaffe Fighter-Bombers over Britain* (2003)

Hastings and St Leonards Observer, *Hastings and St Leonards in the Front Line* (1945)

Lampe, D., *The Last Ditch* (1968)

Mace, M.F., *They Also Served – The Story of Sussex Lifeboats at War* (2001)

Matanle, I., *World War Two* (1997)

Ogly, B., *Doodlebugs and Rockets* (1992)

Peak, S., *Fishermen of Hastings* (1985)

Poulsom, N., Rumble, M. and Smith, K., *Sussex Police Forces* (1987)

Ramsey, W., *The Blitz Then and Now, Vol. 1* (1987)

Ramsey, W., *The Blitz Then and Now, Vol. 2* (1988)

Ramsey, W., *The Blitz Then and Now, Vol. 3* (1990)

Rowland, D., *Spitfires over Sussex* (2000)

Winslow, T., *Forewarned is Forearmed* (1948)

INDEX

Page numbers in **bold** refer to illustrations

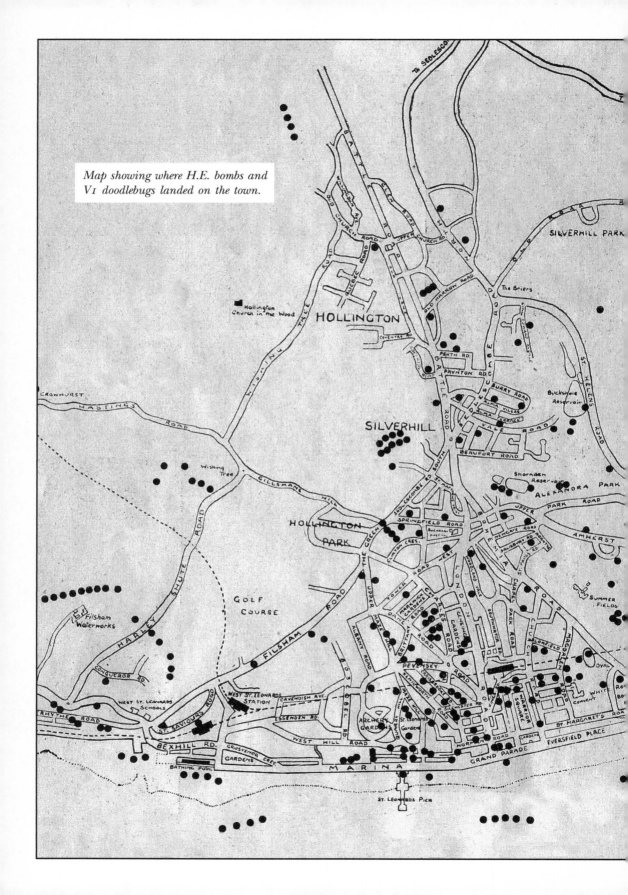

Map showing where H.E. bombs and VI doodlebugs landed on the town.